MEDITATIONS
of EPICTETUS

THE SLAVE WHO
FREED KINGS

MEDITATIONS
of EPICTITUS

THE SLAVE WHO FREED KINGS

ISBN: 978-1-997672-04-3 for ISP Global Design Publishing | Studio Second Edition, April 2025

Disclaimer: This book is intended to provide general information and inspiration based on the author's personal experiences, observations, and interpretations. It is not a substitute for professional advice or treatment. The author and publisher disclaim any liability in connection with the use of this information.

Written by Natalie Larsen | Researched by Oliver Michaels

Global Design Publishing | © 2024

TABLE OF CONTENTS

A Special Note from the Author

A Note Regarding Meditations and interpretations written nearly 2,000 years ago.

This book invites readers to approach stoicism reflections on virtue and humanity with an understanding of their universal relevance. In ancient texts, the term "man" was commonly employed as a general reference, encompassing both men and women in discussions of human nature, virtue, and ethical conduct. This linguistic convention reflected the philosophical norms of the time, where "man" symbolized humankind as a whole rather than indicating gender exclusivity.

Greek and Latin sources often used terms like anthropos or homo to denote humanity collectively, illustrating that these reflections applied to all individuals—any who sought to embody wisdom, integrity, and moral virtue.

In this translation, we honor this historical context by recognizing that "man" in these teachings represents all of humanity. The wisdom of Epictitus and Marcus Aurelius reaches across both gender lines, underscoring the mutual appreciation and strength between men and women who strive to live virtuously. By extending this inclusive spirit to readers today, we affirm that the pursuit of goodness, resilience, and self-mastery is a shared endeavor—one that remains as relevant now as it was nearly two thousand years ago. My goal here is to verify that Stoicism was written for both men and women, and I want it to be welcomed and enjoyed equally.

N Larsen

Foreword

The Slave Who Freed Kings

Foreword by Oliver Michaels

In hidden corners of ancient texts and the faded ink of forgotten manuscripts, historian Natalie Larsen uncovered what would become one of the most stirring journeys of her career. This journey, which began with a quest to understand the raw essence of Stoicism, would bring her face-to-face with timeless wisdom through two towering figures: Marcus Aurelius, the philosopher-king, and Epictetus, the enslaved philosopher who inspired Aurelius and liberated minds across empires.

At the heart of these discoveries lay Méric Casaubon's early 1634 translations of Aurelius' *Meditations*, which revealed a Marcus Aurelius few had seen: not just the stoic emperor in full command, but a man intimately familiar with questions, doubt, fear, and weariness. Larsen's discoveries that Casaubon's work opened a window into the inner life of a leader who, despite wielding immense power, found himself vulnerable to the same struggles that haunt us all.

Epictetus taught that true freedom lies not in escaping our circumstances but in mastering our inner world.

Marcus Aurelius had written these notes as a private sanctuary, a dialogue with himself to strengthen his spirit. These reflections were never meant to be read by others, yet through Casaubon's meticulous translations, we glimpse the humanity behind one of Rome's greatest leaders.

This exploration of Stoic thought led Larsen further back, to one of the foundational voices in Stoicism—Epictetus. Epictetus taught that true freedom lies not in escaping our circumstances but in mastering our inner world.

> *..a collection of writings titled Discourses, Arrian faithfully recorded Epictetus' lessons, preserving not only the philosophy but the spirit of a teacher who inspired kings, emperors, and philosophers alike.*

He knew the meaning of hardship intimately, having been born into slavery, and his teachings reached those who could not be further from his origins: the Emperor Kings of Rome.

It was Arrian, Epictetus' devoted pupil, who preserved the very essence of these teachings, ensuring their survival for centuries. In a collection of writings titled *Discourses*, Arrian faithfully recorded Epictetus' lessons, preserving not only the philosophy but the spirit of a teacher who inspired kings, emperors, and philosophers alike. Arrian captured the clarity of Epictetus' voice and the urgency of his message—one that calls each of us to rise above both hardship and privilege. Through Arrian's dedicated transcriptions, we hear Epictetus' voice urging us to free ourselves from the prisons of overthinking, from anxieties, and from the cycles of suffering that keep us bound.

This book, *The Slave Who Freed Kings*, is an extraordinary exploration of Epictetus' and Marcus Aurelius' wisdom through Historian Natalie Larsen's research, interwoven with the precision and depth of Casaubon's and Arrian's insights. Together, these voices create a symphony of wisdom that resonates across time, speaking to our deepest fears, our loftiest ideals, and our most human struggles.

What emerges from Larsens work is a profound and original Stoicism—a philosophy not simply for the learned, but for every human seeking freedom from doubt, fear, and division. Epictetus' teachings, born of hardship and captured through Arrian's devotion, and Marcus Aurelius' reflections, then preserved by Casaubon's translations, offer a toolkit for transformation. They invite us not to escape life's struggles, but to confront them with courage, resilience, and inner strength.

As you read, you will be guided by the teachings of a slave who freed the minds of kings and by a king who found peace within his own uncertainties. This book brings Stoicism to life, showing how this philosophy—born in ancient times—remains one of the most powerful and inspiring guides for our present world and for humanity's next two thousand years.

Introduction

The Journey of Epictetus –

The Origins of Wisdom

In the ancient city of Hierapolis, nestled in what is now modern-day Turkey, a child was born into a world that held no freedom for him. Epictetus, whose name means "acquired" or "gained," came into existence as property rather than as a person, destined for a life of servitude under the Roman Empire. He was born a slave, physically constrained and subject to the whims of others.

Yet, even within the walls of his captivity, Epictetus became free in a way that few ever achieve. His spirit, guided by the profound teachings of Stoic philosophy, soared beyond the limitations of his physical reality, paving a path that would not only transform his own life but would also serve as a beacon of resilience, inner strength, and wisdom for generations to come.

This is the story of a man who transcended his chains to become one of history's most influential philosophers. *The Freed Slave Who Taught Kings* is not merely a historical account;

it is an exploration of freedom in its most essential form, a journey through the life and teachings of Epictetus, who proved that true liberation comes from within. In a world that is more polarized and chaotic than ever, Epictetus' wisdom resonates across the millennia, offering us tools to navigate our own internal and external battles. This book invites you into Epictetus' world, showing you not only how he conquered his own mind but also how his teachings continue to offer a path to resilience and integrity amid the noise and division of modern life.

Part 1: The Journey of Epictetus – Origins of Wisdom draws us back to Epictetus' beginnings, inviting readers to walk alongside him as he discovers, and ultimately masters, Stoic principles that would shape the rest of his life. But more than a simple recounting of events, this journey reveals how Stoicism was not just a philosophy for Epictetus; it was his survival. Born into a system designed to break the human spirit, he found a way to remain whole by embracing principles that turned his limitations into his greatest strengths. His journey is a testament to the Stoic idea that while external circumstances may be beyond our control, the inner landscape of the mind remains ours alone to command.

Epictetus' Early Life: Freedom in Captivity

Imagine, for a moment, the life of a child who knows only confinement and obedience, with every choice made by another. Epictetus' early life was marked by deprivation and hardship. It is said that he suffered from a physical disability, possibly the result of abuse, which caused him to walk with difficulty. Yet, instead of feeling resentful or broken, Epictetus learned early on to turn his attention inward. He found freedom not in the world around him, but in the sanctuary of his own mind. In the silence of his thoughts, Epictetus discovered a form of independence that would remain unshaken by the hardships he faced.

It was this discovery that led him to Stoicism—a philosophy rooted in the idea that the path to a virtuous life lies in mastering one's own reactions, thoughts, and desires. As he grew, Epictetus came under the mentorship of Musonius Rufus, a Stoic philosopher who saw the potential within him. Even as a slave, Epictetus was granted the opportunity to study Stoic principles, and it was here that he began to understand that power was not determined by one's social status, but by the ability to control one's own mind.

This philosophy was no abstract concept for Epictetus; it was a practical guide for survival. In Stoicism, he found a discipline that allowed him to bear his burdens with grace, a philosophy that taught him to accept what he could not change while remaining resolute in the face of adversity. Epictetus came to embody the Stoic ideal of inner freedom—an independence that could not be touched by the chains that bound his body.

From Slavery to Influence: The Power of a Philosopher's Words

As fate would have it, Epictetus eventually gained his freedom, likely after the death of Emperor Nero, under whom his master, Epaphroditus, had served. Free from physical bondage, Epictetus dedicated his life to teaching Stoicism, not just as a philosopher, but as one who had lived it in its most profound form. He established a school in Rome, where he taught young minds and seasoned scholars alike, emphasizing the power of self-control, virtue, and inner peace. His words spread through the Roman Empire, reaching not only his students but also future generations who would find solace in his teachings.

Yet, Epictetus' life took another turn when Emperor Domitian began to view philosophers as potential threats, banishing them from Rome. Once again, Epictetus faced exile. But rather than viewing this as a setback, he accepted his circumstances with the calm resilience that had defined his life thus far. Moving to Nicopolis, in Greece, he rebuilt his school and continued to teach. It was here that his student, Arrian of Nicomedia, meticulously transcribed Epictetus' lessons, preserving them in what would become *The Discourses* and *The Enchiridion (The Handbook)*—two of the most important works in Stoic literature.

Arrian's dedication to preserving Epictetus' teachings cannot be overstated. Himself a noted historian and philosopher, Arrian recorded Epictetus' words with a devotion to authenticity, aiming to capture not only the content of the teachings but also the essence of Epictetus' spirit. In doing so, Arrian ensured that Epictetus' philosophy would survive long after his death, offering guidance to anyone seeking strength, peace, and purpose.

A Legacy That Touched Kings and Generations Beyond

One of those touched by Epictetus' words was none other than the Roman Emperor Marcus Aurelius, whose own reflections on Stoicism would become the revered text known as *Meditations*. Although they never met, Epictetus' teachings profoundly shaped Marcus' approach to life and leadership. This connection between the freed slave and the emperor speaks to the universal appeal of Stoic philosophy: wisdom is not confined by social standing, power, or wealth. The virtues

Epictetus upheld—integrity, resilience, and inner freedom—resonate as powerfully today as they did in the halls of Rome.

Epictetus' teachings are not relics of the past. In a world that is increasingly defined by external validation, endless distractions, and polarizing opinions, his call to look inward, to find strength within oneself, is more relevant than ever. He teaches us that while we may have little control over the chaos around us, we have absolute control over how we respond to it. In his philosophy, we find a timeless guide to navigating life with courage, discipline, and compassion.

The Journey Awaits: A Modern Path Through Ancient Wisdom

This book will take you through Epictetus' teachings with the same devotion that Arrian exhibited in preserving them. Part 1, *The Journey of Epictetus – Origins of Wisdom,* unveils the early life, challenges, and triumphs of a man who overcame the constraints of his time, embodying the Stoic ideals that have made his philosophy a cornerstone of personal resilience. It will show you how Stoicism became not just a set of beliefs for Epictetus, but a means of survival and a path to freedom.

In the chapters that follow, you will see how Epictetus' teachings on control, acceptance, and virtue have shaped centuries of thought and how they apply to the complexities of today's world. From managing overthinking and anxiety to building resilience in a divisive society, Epictetus' insights offer more than ancient wisdom—they offer a practical framework for inner peace.

As you embark on this journey, remember that Epictetus' life is not merely a story of survival against the odds. It is a testament to the power of the mind, a reminder that no matter our circumstances, the freedom to shape our thoughts, actions, and reactions lies within each of us. May his teachings inspire you to find your own path to resilience, integrity, and true freedom, just as they have inspired countless others across history.

"Never let the future disturb you. You will meet it,
if you have to, with the same weapons of reason
which today arm you against the present."

—Marcus Aurelius

Chapter 1

Born into Slavery, Free in Spirit Ancient Wisdom

In the bustling city of Hierapolis, against the pale limestone terraces and the warmth of ancient stone, a young boy toiled under the weight of a life he had not chosen. His name was Epictetus, meaning "acquired" or "gained"—not a name born of love or legacy, but a label reflecting his status as property.

He was a child in bondage, and his earliest memories were of labor and submission, of being watched with disdain by masters who saw him as no more than an asset, something to be used, to be ordered, to be worked.

Hierapolis, the city of his birth, was a strange blend of beauty and oppression. Known for its healing hot springs and gleaming white cliffs, it was a destination for the affluent, for pilgrims who sought physical relief from the same mineral-rich waters that would never touch the lips of slaves. Epictetus would have watched them pass by, those free citizens of Rome who came in search of health, while he endured a life where even the simple privilege of moving freely was denied.

But Epictetus was not merely born a slave. From an early age, he endured the harsh reality of a physical limitation—a condition that left his leg crippled, forcing him to walk with pain, his movements forever marked by a limp that no doctor would tend to. Some say his injury was inflicted by his master, Epaphroditus, a freedman who served under Emperor Nero, a master notorious for his cruelty and selfishness. Others suggest it was congenital, a burden he was born with, making his fate seem doubly cruel. Whatever its origin, the injury became part of him, shaping his experience of the world as he learned to endure not only the trials of servitude but also the constant, unrelenting pain of his own body.

"He knew he could not change his status or his leg,
nor could he control the whims of his master. What he
could do was control his mind."

In these early years, Epictetus' life was a symphony of hardships. He was surrounded by power, wealth, and influence, yet he had none of it. And yet, even within these constraints, a seed of something unbreakable was taking root. The other slaves whispered about him, sensing that his gaze was somehow different, that behind his weary eyes lay an intellect too keen, a spirit too undaunted by his suffering. There was something about the way he observed the world, an attentiveness that seemed beyond his years. Epictetus was not content to suffer passively; he began to see his hardship not as a punishment, but as an opportunity to understand himself, to understand life.

As he grew older, Epictetus found himself often alone with his thoughts, searching for ways to escape the agony of his condition. But it wasn't escape in the usual sense he sought. He knew he could not change his status or his leg, nor could he control the whims of his master. What he could do was control his mind. In these silent, solitary reflections, Epictetus began to wrestle with a radical idea: that his freedom lay not in the physical world, but in his own mind.

The Emergence of Inner Freedom

The realization came gradually, like the sun rising inch by inch over the hills of Hierapolis, spreading light where there was once only darkness. Epictetus started to understand that while his body was bound, his mind could roam free.

….With time, Epictetus would come to embody the Stoic idea that "it's not what happens to you, but how you react that matters."

He began to practice detachment, observing his pain, his limitations, even his anger, with a growing sense of distance. Pain was there, yes, but he could choose how to perceive it. The cruelties he faced were present, yet he could determine their power over him.

His thoughts turned inward, finding solace and strength in what he could control—his judgments, his reactions, his attitude toward his suffering. With time, Epictetus would come to embody the Stoic idea that "it's not what happens to you, but how you react that matters." This understanding was not simply intellectual for him; it was survival. Each day that he mastered his response to pain, to indignity, to exhaustion, was a day he claimed a piece of his freedom.

He would think, "The chains may bind my limbs, but they cannot bind my mind."

But how does one practice freedom in chains? For Epictetus, it meant renouncing the need to control things outside himself. If he could not change his status or his disability, he would change the way he thought about them. The world around him was harsh, but he began to see himself as an observer of his own experience, watching his suffering from a place of detachment and resilience. The realization was a revelation, a glimmer of freedom shining brightly within him.

What others called a curse—his disability, his slavery—Epictetus began to see as his training ground, the crucible in which his spirit was being forged.

As he matured, Epictetus found his own way of reflecting on this newfound power. He would think, "The chains may bind my limbs, but they cannot bind my mind." This was the mantra that formed in his heart, a creed that grew stronger with each challenge, each new trial. What others called a curse—his disability, his slavery—Epictetus began to see as his training ground, the crucible in which his spirit was being forged.

The Influence of Stoic Thought

Around this time, Epictetus was introduced to the teachings of Musonius Rufus, a Roman philosopher known for his powerful convictions and adherence to Stoic principles. Musonius was a man of deep integrity, one who saw beyond wealth and status to the essence of a person's character. Despite Epictetus' status as a slave, Musonius noticed something remarkable in him—a drive, a resilience that defied his circumstances. He granted Epictetus the rare privilege of studying philosophy, a gift that changed the course of Epictetus' life.

Under Musonius' guidance, Epictetus began to formalize the Stoic principles he had been intuitively practicing. He learned that the Stoics believed in focusing on what one could control—one's thoughts, judgments, and actions—while accepting what one could not. This was not new to Epictetus;

he had lived these principles, not because of choice, but because his circumstances demanded it. Yet, in studying Stoicism, he found the words and ideas to articulate his understanding.

Stoicism became not only a belief system but a way of being, a means of transforming suffering into strength.

For Epictetus, these teachings were transformative. He no longer had to search for answers alone; the Stoic texts became his companions, his solace. They told him that he was not powerless, that his worth lay not in his status or his physical condition, but in his character. Stoicism did not promise to end his suffering, but it offered him a way to suffer nobly, to find purpose and strength in the very challenges that others would flee.

Freedom Within the Mind's Walls

As Epictetus continued to study, the lines between his life and his philosophy began to blur. Stoicism became not only a belief system but a way of being, a means of transforming suffering into strength. His reflections grew deeper, his spirit more resilient. His life as a slave might continue, but he knew now that his spirit was free.

...in that moment, he understood what true freedom was. It was not a matter of place or possession, of wealth or title. Freedom, he saw, was the quiet resolve within, the ability to remain steady, unshaken by the storms of life.

Epictetus began to realize that true power came from the mind's ability to choose its response. In moments of physical pain or humiliation, he would remind himself that these were only surface realities, external forces with no bearing on his inner world. His disability, once a source of bitterness, became almost incidental to his identity, a challenge rather than a curse. When his master would look down on him or bark orders, Epictetus would think, "These are but shadows; they cannot touch the light within."

One evening, after a long day of labor, Epictetus looked out over the city. The skyline was fading, bathed in the red glow of dusk. And in that moment, he understood what true freedom was. It was not a matter of place or possession, of wealth or title. Freedom, he saw, was the quiet resolve within, the ability to remain steady, unshaken by the storms of life. For as long as he could choose his response, he could endure anything. This understanding became his shield, a source of strength that no man, not even his master, could take from him.

Beyond the Chains: The Birth of a Philosopher

Epictetus' journey was only beginning. In the years to come, he would continue to develop his thoughts, to find new depths within himself. His mind became his refuge, his freedom. His suffering did not disappear, but he became the master of it, rather than its victim. And in mastering his own mind, Epictetus found the foundation of the philosophy that would one day influence emperors and scholars alike.

Born into chains, Epictetus had discovered a freedom that few would ever know—a freedom that no empire could conquer, a strength that no physical limitation could diminish. He learned that the truest form of liberty came not from the outside world but from within. And it was here, in the quiet revolution of his mind, that he began to see himself not as a slave, but as a philosopher, a man who would one day teach others that the key to enduring any hardship lies not in changing one's circumstances but in transforming one's spirit.

This understanding would become his legacy. Epictetus, once a nameless slave in Hierapolis, would go on to inspire generations with his teachings, his wisdom, and his indomitable spirit. For in the end, he had shown that the deepest freedom, the one that matters most, can only be found within.

Chapter 2

The Road to Stoicism

In the shadow of the grand Roman Empire, where power and wealth were hoarded by a privileged few and suffering was the lot of many, Epictetus found himself at a crossroads. He had tasted inner freedom, tasted the strange liberation that came not from changing his circumstances but from changing his mind. Yet he still yearned for something more—an anchor, a guide that could give form and clarity to his growing understanding of resilience and control. That guide would come from a man who, though freeborn, was no stranger to hardship and conviction: Musonius Rufus, the philosopher who would ignite in Epictetus a life-long commitment to the Stoic path.

Musonius Rufus was a revered philosopher, one of the most respected Stoics of his time. He was known throughout Rome as a teacher who valued not only knowledge but character, a man who taught that virtue was not just to be studied but to be practiced. Musonius held that philosophy was not simply a matter of intellectual understanding but of daily living, of applying wisdom to one's actions with unwavering dedication. In him, Epictetus saw someone who understood suffering, who saw strength not as something innate, but as something cultivated through perseverance, humility, and a commitment to the highest ideals.

But it was not just fate that brought Epictetus into the orbit of Musonius Rufus. Epaphroditus, his master, had long since recognized a sharpness in Epictetus—a curiosity, an unbreakable resilience. And while Epaphroditus was ruthless and self-serving, he was also pragmatic. He saw value in allowing Epictetus to study under Musonius, to shape the mind that could one day serve his own ambitions. So, in an unusual twist of fortune, Epictetus was granted permission to attend the lectures of Musonius Rufus, stepping into the rarefied world of philosophical discourse that few slaves would ever touch.

For Epictetus, that first meeting with Musonius was transformative. Musonius was a man who embodied Stoicism in every aspect of his life, a figure of serenity and resolve whose wisdom seemed to radiate with an intensity that Epictetus had never encountered. Musonius spoke of the purpose of philosophy as a tool not to escape life, but to engage with it more deeply. He talked of virtue, of living in harmony with nature, and of accepting what life presented—both good and ill—with equanimity. For Epictetus, these teachings were not just ideas but revelations that mirrored the hard-won truths he had come to realize through his own suffering.

The First Lessons in Stoicism

Musonius began his teachings with a foundation that was at once practical and profound. Philosophy, he insisted, was not an abstract endeavor reserved for the idle elite. Rather, it was a discipline, a way of training the mind and soul to respond to the hardships of life with courage and clarity. In the grand forum where Musonius lectured, Epictetus sat among free men and nobles, yet the words spoken seemed directed to him alone.

"Remember this," Musonius would say, his voice calm yet unyielding, "the essence of philosophy is in what we do, not in what we say." And Musonius lived this truth, practicing what he preached with a commitment that was visible to all who followed him. He rejected luxuries, choosing simplicity, and focused on self-discipline, a stark contrast to the indulgent ways of Rome. This asceticism resonated deeply with Epictetus, for he too had learned that strength lay not in the possession of comforts but in the ability to endure their absence.

Epictetus felt as though he had found a language for what he had long felt but could not articulate. Musonius' teachings on the dichotomy of control—of focusing only on what lay within one's power and releasing what lay beyond it—felt like a philosophy of freedom. For a slave, this concept was revolutionary. In a world where his body and labor were owned by another, here was a truth that could never be taken from him. The locus of control lay not in external conditions, but in his own mind.

Yet for all their wealth, these men and women often seemed enslaved to their own desires, perpetually seeking satisfaction yet rarely finding it.

Through Musonius, Epictetus learned that suffering itself could be an instructor. Pain, loss, hardship—these were not to be shunned or feared but to be embraced as opportunities to cultivate resilience. "Do not waste your pain," Musonius would say, a phrase that lingered in Epictetus' mind. Suffering was not an obstacle to virtue but a means by which virtue was tested and strengthened. Epictetus had already begun to understand this on an intuitive level, but through Musonius' teachings, he began to see suffering as a process of refinement, a fire that burned away the impurities of weakness, pride, and resentment, leaving only the strength of character.

Roman Society and Stoic Influence

As Epictetus immersed himself in Stoic philosophy, he also became acutely aware of the world around him. The Roman Empire, with all its grandeur and opulence, was a society of extremes. Power and privilege were concentrated in the hands of a few, while the majority lived lives of toil and uncertainty. The elite indulged in luxuries, seeking pleasure as if it were the very essence of life. Yet for all their wealth, these men and women often seemed enslaved to their own desires, perpetually seeking satisfaction yet rarely finding it.

In this world, Stoicism presented a radical alternative. The Stoics held that true happiness did not come from wealth or pleasure but from living in accordance with nature and reason. They valued self-discipline, virtue, and an inner freedom that transcended material circumstances. Musonius himself was a model of this ideal, and his disdain for excesses became a source of quiet tension in a society that viewed wealth as the ultimate symbol of success. Through him, Epictetus learned that there was more strength in self-restraint than in indulgence, more power in mastering oneself than in ruling over others.

As Epictetus absorbed these teachings, he began to see the disparities around him with new eyes. The very men who commanded armies, who held sway over lives, seemed weaker than the poor and humble. For while they were rich in power, they were impoverished in spirit, slaves to their appetites, their fears, their endless need for validation. And here lay the great paradox of Stoicism in the Roman world: it offered freedom not through possession but through renunciation, through the mastery of oneself rather than dominion over others.

The world of Stoicism and the values of Rome were often at odds. Rome prized conquest, control, and the relentless pursuit of glory, while Stoicism urged humility, self-control, and harmony with nature. To be a Stoic in such a society was, in many ways, a rebellion against its very core. And for Epictetus, whose life was already a testament to resilience, this philosophical rebellion became a guiding force.

Epictetus' Inner Transformation

Musonius Rufus became not just a teacher to Epictetus but a mirror, reflecting back to him the wisdom and strength he had long cultivated in silence. Through Musonius, Epictetus learned to formalize his insights, to structure his thoughts in a way that would form the foundation of his own teachings. He began to see that the self-mastery he had practiced out of necessity was, in fact, the heart of Stoic philosophy. Epictetus' experiences as a slave gave him a unique lens through which he could understand and embody Stoic teachings, allowing him to delve into its depths in ways that even free men might struggle to comprehend.

Stoicism taught Epictetus to see beyond his own suffering, to recognize that pain was transient, a mere surface experience that could not touch the soul unless allowed. His physical limitations, once a source of frustration, became almost inconsequential. Instead of bemoaning his injury, he began to see it as a lesson in patience and humility, a constant reminder of the body's frailty and the soul's strength. With each lesson, he grew in conviction, embracing the idea that he was, in a sense, unconquerable. For how could he be harmed if he did not allow harm to reach his inner self?

As the seasons passed, Epictetus became one of Musonius' most devoted students, absorbing each teaching with an intensity born of personal need. He did not learn Stoicism simply as a philosophy but as a way of life. He meditated on the idea that virtue was its own reward, that no external condition could diminish the worth of a person who lived in harmony with reason and nature. And as he grew in understanding, he began to develop his own insights, insights that would one day be passed on to generations as timeless truths.

The Formative Teachings of Musonius Rufus

One of the most profound lessons that Musonius imparted to Epictetus was the idea of 'living according to nature.' To the Stoics, nature was not merely the physical world but a guiding principle, a force that encompassed reason, virtue, and the natural order of life. Musonius taught that to live well was to align oneself with this principle, to cultivate virtues like courage, justice, temperance, and wisdom. These were not merely ideals but practices, qualities to be nurtured daily, in every choice, every action.

Epictetus embraced these teachings, finding in them a purpose that transcended his circumstances. He began to view himself not as a slave bound by his master's commands, but as a student bound by the pursuit of virtue. His daily life became an exercise in Stoic discipline. When his leg ached or his master demanded his labor, Epictetus would remind himself that these were only external pressures. What mattered was how he chose to respond. He could either view them as sources of suffering or as opportunities to strengthen his resolve.

Another cornerstone of Musonius' teaching was the Stoic understanding of "indifference." To the Stoic, things like wealth, health, and social status were indifferent—they held no intrinsic value. Epictetus learned to see that while society placed high value on power and wealth, these things were ultimately meaningless if they did not serve the purpose of virtue. This understanding gave Epictetus a new perspective on his own life. His status as a slave, his lack of wealth, his physical disability—these were all indifferent. They did not define him, nor did they diminish his worth.

As his understanding deepened, Epictetus found a profound sense of peace. He was, in a sense, free—free in a way that no slave could have imagined, free in a way that even his master was not. For Epictetus had come to realize that true freedom lay not in the ability to act without constraint but in the mastery of one's own mind. He had learned that a person who could control their thoughts and reactions was untouchable, invulnerable to the whims of fate and the cruelties of men.

A Life Forever Changed

Through Musonius Rufus, Epictetus had found a path that was both liberating and demanding, a philosophy that challenged him to rise above his circumstances and live with dignity and purpose. Musonius' teachings were not simply a balm for his suffering; they were a call to greatness, a summons to live as a philosopher in the truest sense. Epictetus' heart and mind had been transformed, his understanding of himself reshaped by the Stoic ideal.

In this transformation, Epictetus found the roots of the philosophy that would one day bear his name. For while he had learned from Musonius, he would soon forge his own path, deepening and refining his beliefs until they became his own. He was, after all, not merely a student but a man who had tested these truths in the fires of adversity. And in doing so, he had become a living testament to the power of Stoicism—a man who had found freedom not in the world but in himself.

In the years to come, Epictetus would continue to build on these teachings, to develop them into a philosophy that would resonate with emperors, scholars, and ordinary men alike. His journey with Musonius Rufus was only the beginning, the first step on a road that would lead him to become one of history's greatest Stoic philosophers, a man who understood, perhaps better than anyone, that the road to wisdom begins not in power or privilege, but in the courage to seek freedom within.

Chapter 3a

Exile and the Legacy of Wisdom

For Epictetus, the path to wisdom was marked by hardship and transformation. Born into slavery and later freed, Epictetus was no stranger to the limitations of human life. His early years were defined by the boundaries others placed upon him, the restrictions of being controlled by the will of another. Yet, even after gaining freedom, Epictetus remained exposed to the harsh realities of the world. His status and security were fragile, subject to the tides of Roman politics. And when Emperor Domitian decreed that all philosophers should be expelled from Rome, Epictetus once again found himself in circumstances beyond his control, exiled from the heart of the empire he had called home. However, what might have been seen as a punishment, a forced retreat, Epictetus chose to embrace as an opportunity. For Epictetus, exile became a crucible that refined his understanding of freedom, resilience, and wisdom.

Exile took Epictetus to Nicopolis, a city on the western coast of Greece. Stripped of the familiarity and comfort of Rome, he faced a new challenge: to establish a life and purpose in a place where he was, once again, a stranger. This period of exile could have embittered a lesser person, but Epictetus had spent his life developing a perspective that valued mental freedom over physical liberty. For him, freedom was an internal state, something no decree, no exile, and no circumstance could take away. In Nicopolis, Epictetus was able to put this belief into practice, using his isolation from Roman society as a chance to deepen his understanding of Stoic philosophy.

Instead of viewing exile as a setback, Epictetus saw it as a chance to establish a legacy grounded in resilience and intellectual freedom. Rather than retreating into bitterness or despair, he chose to focus on his inner life, refining his thoughts and principles, and ultimately establishing a philosophical school. Nicopolis became his new center of learning, a sanctuary where he could share the teachings that had shaped him with those who sought wisdom and guidance. The school quickly gained a reputation for its rigorous training in philosophy, attracting students from various parts of the ancient world who were drawn to Epictetus' emphasis on mental freedom and resilience. Here, Epictetus taught that life's hardships were not obstacles but opportunities, that freedom was not a matter of external circumstance but of internal mastery.

Epictetus' school in Nicopolis was different from many other schools of the time. It was not simply a place for intellectual discourse or debate but a center for personal transformation. Epictetus demanded more than intellectual understanding from his students; he demanded that they live out the principles they studied. Philosophy, he taught, was not an abstract pursuit but a way of life. His lessons focused on cultivating inner resilience, on training the mind to remain steady and clear even amidst life's storms. He emphasized that true wisdom lay in understanding what one can control and accepting what one cannot, a teaching that resonated all the more profoundly given his own experiences of slavery and exile.

In his classroom, Epictetus shared not only Stoic teachings but also his personal experiences, using his life as an example of the principles he taught. His own hardships lent credibility to his words; students saw that Epictetus was not merely espousing philosophical theories but was living out the values he taught. Through him, they learned that adversity could be a powerful teacher, that freedom was found not in escaping difficulties but in confronting them with courage and clarity. Epictetus' presence was a testament to the strength of a mind that had been tempered by hardship and refined through adversity.

Epictetus taught his students that while the world might be unpredictable, their inner lives could remain untouched by external forces. His lessons emphasized self-mastery, the idea that one's mind was a sanctuary, a place where true freedom could always be found. He taught that suffering did not come from events themselves but from our judgments about them. In Nicopolis, Epictetus' philosophy took on a new depth, as he emphasized that even in exile, one could be free. To Epictetus, freedom was not a matter of physical location or social status but of the choices one made in response to life's challenges.

This period of exile allowed Epictetus to become not just a teacher but a sage, a guide who could lead others to discover freedom within themselves. His school became a haven for students seeking wisdom, a place where they could learn to cultivate inner peace and resilience. Epictetus' lessons on freedom, resilience, and self-mastery resonated deeply with his students, offering them a philosophy that was both practical and transformative. He taught that by focusing on what lies within our control—our own thoughts, responses, and actions—we gain a sense of peace and purpose that no external event can disrupt.

As his teachings spread, Epictetus began to attract students who were not only interested in Stoic philosophy but were profoundly moved by his personal story. They came to learn not just from his words but from his example, to see how a man who had experienced both slavery and exile could live with a sense of peace and purpose. Through his school, Epictetus created a legacy that would endure far beyond the city of Nicopolis. He was not just teaching a philosophy; he was embodying it, showing his students that true freedom is found in the strength of one's own mind.

In Nicopolis, Epictetus had turned exile into an opportunity for growth, a chance to deepen his understanding of Stoic principles and to live them out with conviction. His school became a place where students could learn to navigate life's challenges with resilience, where they could discover that freedom lies not in escaping difficulty but in facing it with a steady mind and an open heart. Epictetus' exile had refined his teachings into a philosophy of strength, one not dictated by circumstance but crafted through self-mastery. His school had become a haven for those seeking wisdom, where students would soon come to learn that true freedom lies not in avoiding adversity but in embracing it with a steady mind.

"You have power over your mind—not outside events. Realize this, and you will find strength."

—Marcus Aurelius

Chapter 3b

Arrian's Legacy

For Arrian of Nicomedia, the journey to Nicopolis was more than a pilgrimage; it was the beginning of a profound transformation. A young man of promising intellect and ambition, Arrian had already begun to make a name for himself as a historian and philosopher. Yet, despite his accomplishments, he was searching for something more—a philosophy that could anchor him in a world marked by unpredictability and change. He found that anchor in Epictetus, a philosopher whose teachings on freedom, resilience, and self-mastery spoke to Arrian's deepest longings. What began as intellectual curiosity grew into a lifelong devotion, a commitment to preserve and share Epictetus' wisdom with future generations.

Arrian found himself not merely studying philosophy but experiencing a transformation in how he understood the world and his place within it.

When Arrian first arrived at Epictetus' school, he was struck by the atmosphere. The school was not a grand academy or a lavish temple of learning, but a simple setting where students gathered to learn from a man who had faced life's most profound hardships. Epictetus himself was a figure who radiated calm and strength, a man whose physical limitations seemed inconsequential compared to the power of his mind. Arrian was captivated, not only by the teachings but by the man himself, a philosopher who embodied the principles he taught. Epictetus' emphasis on inner freedom, the idea that one's mind could remain unshaken by external circumstances, resonated deeply with Arrian. Here was a philosophy not confined to theory but lived in practice, a philosophy that had been forged in the fires of adversity and refined through experience.

Under Epictetus' guidance, Arrian found himself not merely studying philosophy but experiencing a transformation in how he understood the world and his place within it. Epictetus taught that true freedom was a matter of internal mastery, that one's peace did not depend on the shifting tides of fate but on the strength of one's own mind. Arrian absorbed these teachings, realizing that they offered a way to live with resilience and purpose, even in the face of uncertainty. He saw in Epictetus a mentor whose wisdom was not bound by time or circumstance, a guide who could help him navigate the complexities of life with clarity and integrity.

As Arrian's understanding of Stoicism deepened, so did his admiration for Epictetus. He recognized that Epictetus' philosophy was a gift not only to those who could attend his school but to all who sought wisdom. Arrian became increasingly aware of the importance of preserving Epictetus' teachings, of ensuring that this wisdom would not be lost to time or forgotten in the annals of history. He saw himself not only as a student but as a steward of Epictetus' legacy, someone who could carry these teachings forward and make them accessible to future generations. This realization sparked a sense of duty within him, a commitment to capture the essence of Epictetus' philosophy in writing.

Arrian set out to document Epictetus' teachings with meticulous care, striving to capture not only the content of the lessons but the spirit in which they were given. He observed the way Epictetus spoke, the clarity and conviction with which he conveyed each principle. Epictetus taught with a calm authority, his words shaped by a lifetime of experience and hardship, and Arrian knew that these teachings deserved to be recorded with the utmost fidelity. His writings would not be a personal interpretation or embellishment; they would be a faithful transcription, an effort to present Epictetus' wisdom as closely as possible to how it had been shared in the school at Nicopolis.

In his dedication to preserving Epictetus' teachings, Arrian compiled what would become two of the most influential works of Stoic philosophy: *The Discourses* and the *Enchiridion*. *The Discourses* captured the breadth of Epictetus' teachings, his reflections on the nature of control, the importance of virtue, and the pursuit of inner peace. It provided readers with a comprehensive view of Epictetus' philosophy, a guide for living that addressed the fundamental questions of human existence. The *Enchiridion*, or "Handbook," distilled these teachings into a concise manual, a practical tool for those who sought to incorporate Stoic principles into their daily lives. This handbook would become a cornerstone of Stoic literature, a source of guidance and inspiration for philosophers, statesmen, and seekers of wisdom throughout the centuries.

For Arrian, the act of preserving Epictetus' teachings was a labor of love, a tribute to a teacher who had changed his life. He knew that these writings would serve as a beacon for those seeking to navigate life's challenges with strength and serenity, offering a philosophy that valued freedom of the mind above all else. Arrian's devotion to this task reflects not only his respect for Epictetus but his belief in the timeless relevance of Stoic wisdom. He saw in Epictetus' teachings a path to resilience and peace, a guide to facing adversity with courage and clarity, and he was determined to ensure that this path would remain open for all who wished to follow it.

The relationship between Epictetus and Arrian was more than that of teacher and student; it was a partnership in the pursuit of truth. Arrian's role as the preserver of Epictetus' legacy was one he approached with humility and reverence, aware of the responsibility he bore to future generations. He understood that Epictetus' philosophy was not merely a response to the unique challenges of their time but a universal guide to living well. Through his writings, Arrian ensured that Epictetus' wisdom would reach far beyond the confines of the school in Nicopolis, offering guidance to those who sought freedom, resilience, and inner peace.

In transcribing Epictetus' teachings, Arrian knew he was not simply recording words; he was preserving a legacy of thought, a way of life that transcended the limitations of time and place. Epictetus' philosophy was rooted in his personal experience, in his journey from slavery to freedom, from hardship to wisdom. Arrian saw that this philosophy had the power to transform lives, to provide a foundation of peace and resilience for anyone willing to embrace its teachings. He believed that by preserving Epictetus' words, he was offering future readers a gift—a way to rise above the challenges of life and discover a freedom that no external circumstance could take away.

Through Arrian's dedication, Epictetus' philosophy would endure, guiding countless individuals in the quest for self-mastery and inner strength. The *Discourses* and the *Enchiridion* became more than mere texts; they became conduits of Epictetus' spirit, channels through which his wisdom would flow across generations. Arrian's work ensured that Epictetus' teachings would remain accessible, a source of light and guidance for those navigating the complexities of life. His writings allowed Epictetus' legacy to live on, offering a path to freedom and resilience for all who sought it.

Arrian's commitment to preserving Epictetus' wisdom was a testament to the profound impact that Epictetus had on those around him. Through Arrian's writings, Epictetus' teachings became a beacon for philosophers, leaders, and ordinary individuals alike, offering a philosophy that valued freedom of the mind, integrity, and resilience. This legacy speaks to the enduring relevance of Epictetus' teachings, a reminder that true strength and peace are found not in external circumstances but in the mastery of one's own mind.

In reflecting on Arrian's journey, we see a young philosopher who came to Nicopolis seeking wisdom and left with a mission to share that wisdom with the world. Arrian's devotion to Epictetus' teachings transformed him from a student into a steward of Stoic philosophy, a guardian of a legacy that continues to inspire and guide us today. Through his writings, Arrian ensured that Epictetus' voice would echo across the centuries, offering timeless insights into the nature of freedom, resilience, and inner peace.

As he meticulously transcribed each lesson, Arrian knew that he was not only preserving the teachings of a great philosopher but also honoring the life of a man who had lived those teachings. He understood that Epictetus' wisdom was not simply a set of ideas but a way of life, a path to freedom that anyone could follow. Through the *Discourses* and the *Enchiridion*,

Arrian gave Epictetus' philosophy a voice that would reach far beyond Nicopolis, a voice that would resonate with all who seek to live with purpose, strength, and serenity. Arrian's legacy is a testament to the power of philosophy to transcend time, offering a path to freedom and resilience that remains as relevant today as it was in the days of Epictetus.

Chapter 4

Legacy and Influence on Marcus Aurelius

In the grand lineage of Stoic thought, few figures shine as brightly as Marcus Aurelius, the philosopher-emperor whose reflections on life, power, and virtue continue to inspire people across the world. But while his *Meditations* is often celebrated as a hallmark of Stoic wisdom, its foundation lies in the teachings of a former slave whose own struggles, resilience, and philosophy laid the groundwork for much of Aurelius' understanding of virtue.

This is the story of how Epictetus' influence reached the heart of Rome, shaping not only an emperor's philosophy but also the ethos of an empire. Through Marcus Aurelius, Epictetus' words would echo through history, reminding generations that true power lies not in conquest, but in self-mastery.

The Unlikely Reach of a Philosopher-Slave

The connection between Epictetus and Marcus Aurelius was not one of direct mentorship; they never met, and their lives differed in almost every conceivable way. Epictetus, born into slavery and familiar with the harshest of conditions, had lived with the limitations of a crippled leg and the arbitrary power of masters. Aurelius, on the other hand, was born into privilege, raised within the circles of power and educated under Rome's finest tutors. But it was precisely because of Epictetus' teachings that Stoicism would find its way to Aurelius, providing him with the philosophical strength needed to navigate the tumultuous responsibilities of ruling the vast Roman Empire.

Though separated by decades, the teachings of Epictetus reached Marcus Aurelius through *The Discourses* and *The Enchiridion*—the works preserved by Arrian with unwavering dedication. As a young man, Marcus had been introduced to Stoic philosophy as part of his formal education, and he studied the works of many Stoic thinkers. But Epictetus held a special resonance for him. Here was a man who had lived the philosophy he taught, who had turned suffering into wisdom, who had shown that true power lay not in control over others but in mastery of oneself. Epictetus' words were not theoretical musings; they were the hard-won insights of a man who had endured the worst life had to offer, yet emerged with his spirit unbroken.

For Marcus Aurelius, Epictetus was a reminder that virtue was not the privilege of the elite, but the right of every individual who sought it. Through Epictetus' teachings, Marcus learned that his own role as emperor was not to amass power or command absolute control, but to live with integrity, to rule with humility, and to face hardship with courage. It was a philosophy that would guide him through some of the most challenging periods of his reign and provide him with a framework for handling the responsibilities and burdens of power.

The Impact of Stoicism on Marcus Aurelius' Reign

As Marcus Aurelius ascended to power, he found himself in a position that few philosophers could imagine. The role of emperor was fraught with complexities that tested not only his political acumen but his personal ethics. He faced challenges from every angle: wars on the empire's borders, political intrigue within Rome, and the constant need to balance the welfare of his people with the demands of governance. In such an environment, it would have been easy for a ruler to slip into cynicism or tyranny, to become hardened by the endless pressures of leadership. But Epictetus' teachings provided Marcus with a steadying influence, a set of principles that allowed him to navigate the weight of his responsibilities with integrity.

One of the core lessons Marcus absorbed from Epictetus was the Stoic concept of control—the idea that while external events lay beyond our influence, our reactions to them remain entirely within our power. As an emperor, this principle was both empowering and humbling. He could not dictate the course of battles, the whims of fate, or the loyalty of those around him. But he could control his own actions, his own responses to crises. He could choose to face each challenge with reason and equanimity rather than anger or despair.

In *Meditations,* we see the profound influence of this idea, as Marcus repeatedly reminds himself to focus on his own thoughts and actions rather than the uncontrollable events swirling around him. "You have power over your mind—not outside events," he wrote. "Realize this, and you will find strength." These words echo Epictetus' teaching on the dichotomy of control, showing how deeply the former slave's philosophy had permeated the mind of an emperor.

Epictetus' Influence on Character and Virtue

More than any specific teaching, it was Epictetus' example—his life lived with resilience and dignity—that left a lasting impression on Marcus Aurelius. Epictetus had taught that true virtue lay in living according to one's principles, in acting with honesty, humility, and a sense of duty. For Marcus, this was a powerful guide, especially within the corrupt and often ruthless environment of Roman politics. Epictetus had shown that one could live with integrity even in the most challenging of circumstances, that a person's character was not determined by their status or wealth but by their commitment to virtue.

Inspired by Epictetus, Marcus Aurelius saw his position not as a privilege but as a responsibility, a duty to live by the highest ethical standards and to serve the common good. He approached his role as a philosopher would—questioning his motives, examining his actions, and striving to remain true to his ideals, even when faced with immense pressure to compromise. "Waste no more time arguing about what a good man should be. Be one," he wrote in *Meditations,* encapsulating a lesson that Epictetus himself might have given.

The values that Epictetus instilled in Marcus—humility, integrity, and duty—shaped the way he ruled. Despite the pressures of his office, Marcus avoided the trappings of excess and luxury, preferring simplicity and discipline. He chose not to wield power ruthlessly but to temper it with wisdom, even compassion. In doing so, he offered a rare example of a ruler who sought to embody the virtues he advocated, who understood that the true measure of an emperor was not his wealth or conquests, but his commitment to the welfare of his people.

Meditations: The Emperor's Private Dialogue with Epictetus

In his personal journal, known to us as *Meditations*, Marcus Aurelius recorded his reflections on life, duty, and the Stoic principles that guided him. Though never intended for publication, *Meditations* stands today as one of the most profound works of Stoic philosophy, a text that speaks to the inner life of a man who grappled with the same fears, desires, and moral dilemmas that we all face.

Throughout *Meditations*, the influence of Epictetus is unmistakable. Marcus often echoes his teacher's words, internalizing Epictetus' lessons in ways that reflect both his reverence for the philosopher and his own deep commitment to Stoic principles. When Marcus writes, "The happiness of your life depends upon the quality of your thoughts," he is not merely espousing a philosophical idea—he is speaking as a student of Epictetus, as someone who has internalized the lesson that true freedom is found within.

This dialogue between Marcus and Epictetus, though separated by years, creates a bridge between the philosopher and the emperor. It is a conversation about resilience, about facing life's hardships with grace, and about finding strength in simplicity and self-discipline. Through his reflections, Marcus reveals how Epictetus' teachings became a lifeline, a source of wisdom that allowed him to face the unrelenting pressures of power with dignity and composure.

The Legacy of a Slave's Wisdom

The relationship between Epictetus and Marcus Aurelius illustrates the enduring power of Stoic philosophy—a philosophy that does not recognize social barriers but speaks to the common humanity within each of us. That a former slave could influence an emperor is a testament to the universal relevance of Stoic thought, to its ability to reach across class, circumstance, and time to touch the lives of those who seek it.

> *...without Epictetus, it is unlikely that Marcus would have become the man we know through Meditations.*

Epictetus' legacy, preserved by Arrian and embraced by Marcus Aurelius, became a cornerstone of Stoic thought, a guiding light for anyone who seeks to live with integrity, courage, and inner peace. In his teachings, Marcus found a reminder that even the highest of rulers is bound by the same human struggles as the lowest of subjects. Through Epictetus, Marcus saw that his role as emperor was not a license to indulge in power but a duty to exemplify virtue, to lead by example, and to govern with wisdom and compassion.

Epictetus' Timeless Influence

Today, we remember Marcus Aurelius as a "philosopher-king," a ruler who, against the odds, remained true to his principles. But without Epictetus, it is unlikely that Marcus would have become the man we know through *Meditations*. Epictetus' influence did more than shape an emperor; it preserved the Stoic ethos, ensuring that its wisdom would endure, not as a relic of ancient philosophy but as a living tradition.

Through Marcus Aurelius, Epictetus' teachings reached heights unimaginable for a former slave. They found their way into the minds of countless readers, scholars, and leaders who continue to turn to Stoicism for guidance. And they endure not only in the pages of *Meditations* but in the lives of those who seek freedom through self-mastery, who understand that the truest form of power is the power over oneself.

Epictetus' legacy, made immortal by the dedication of his students and the devotion of Marcus Aurelius, remains a testament to the idea that wisdom transcends status, that virtue is the birthright of all, and that freedom begins within. It is a legacy that speaks across time, a quiet yet powerful reminder that no matter our circumstances, we each have the power to live with purpose, courage, and dignity.

Through Marcus Aurelius, Epictetus lives on—a silent guide who continues to teach that a life of meaning is not defined by what we control, but by how we respond to what lies beyond our control. And in this simple truth lies a wisdom that has, and always will, change lives.

Chapter 5

What You Control and What You Don't

In the quiet spaces of his mind, Epictetus discovered a truth so simple yet so powerful that it would come to form the foundation of Stoic philosophy. He understood that while life throws countless challenges our way—many of which we cannot avoid or predict—the key to peace lies in focusing only on what we can control and releasing what we cannot. This insight, known as the "dichotomy of control," is perhaps Epictetus' most enduring legacy, a teaching that offers not just solace but a blueprint for resilience, calm, and inner freedom.

The dichotomy of control is straightforward yet profound: it is the idea that there are only two types of things in life—those we can control and those we cannot. Epictetus taught that everything external, from the opinions of others to the state of our health, is ultimately beyond our influence. But there is one area that is always within our control: our own mind—our thoughts, choices, and responses. Epictetus believed that if we could learn to focus our energy on this inner domain and release our attachment to external outcomes, we could find a peace unshaken by the turmoil of life.

In this chapter, we'll explore Epictetus' teachings on the dichotomy of control, learning how to identify what is within our power and how to release what lies beyond it. Through specific Stoic techniques such as reframing negative events and practicing acceptance, we will discover how Epictetus' wisdom can transform stress into serenity and make Stoicism not an abstract philosophy but a practical way of living with purpose and calm.

The Dichotomy of Control: A New Lens on Life

Epictetus' teaching on control challenges us to reconsider our relationship with the world. In his work *Enchiridion*, he introduces this concept in its simplest form: "Some things are up to us, and some things are not." These words are often the first lesson taught to those studying Stoicism because they encapsulate a truth that is universal and immediately applicable. The dichotomy of control is not about denying the importance of external events; rather, it's about recognizing where our true power lies.

In practice, this teaching invites us to ask a simple question when facing any challenge or event: Is this something I can control? If the answer is no, then our task is to accept it and move on, directing our energy toward something that we can influence. If the answer is yes, then we focus fully on what we can do, knowing that our peace and happiness depend not on the outcome, but on the integrity of our actions.

Epictetus saw this distinction as the basis for a life of tranquility. He observed that much of our suffering comes not from events themselves, but from our desire to control things that lie beyond our reach. We worry about the opinions of others, stress over future outcomes, and agonize over past events, all of which are beyond our influence. By attempting to control the uncontrollable, we create unnecessary tension and anxiety. But when we shift our focus to what is truly ours—our own thoughts, decisions, and behaviors—we discover a freedom that cannot be shaken.

Letting Go of External Events

One of the most challenging aspects of the dichotomy of control is learning to let go of things that are beyond our influence. This does not mean ignoring them or pretending they don't matter; it means understanding that our well-being does not depend on them. For Epictetus, this was a lesson that required both discipline and practice, and it's one that can transform how we approach everything from our careers to our relationships.

> *a realization that life is unpredictable, that outcomes are uncertain, and that our peace does not depend on what happens to us but on how we choose to respond.*

Consider, for instance, how we often invest emotional energy in outcomes we cannot guarantee. We prepare for a presentation at work and worry about how our colleagues will receive it. We work hard to maintain a relationship, yet fear that our partner's feelings may change. These are natural concerns, but they are also outside our control. Epictetus taught that by focusing on our own actions—preparing as best we can, treating others with kindness, and acting with integrity—we can find peace, regardless of how others respond.

To let go of external events requires a shift in mindset, a willingness to accept that some things will not go our way and that this is not a failure on our part. It is a realization that life is unpredictable, that outcomes are uncertain, and that our peace does not depend on what happens to us but on how we choose to respond. When we learn to release what lies beyond our control, we free ourselves from the constant need to manipulate the world to fit our desires, opening the door to a life of serenity.

Reframing Negative Events: A Stoic Technique

One of the most effective ways to apply the dichotomy of control is through the Stoic practice of reframing negative events. Epictetus believed that our suffering often comes not from the events themselves but from our interpretation of them. In his view, the mind has the power to transform challenges into opportunities for growth, to see setbacks as lessons, and to turn disappointments into a deeper understanding of life.

Reframing is a technique that involves consciously changing the way we view a situation. Instead of seeing a negative event as a catastrophe, we choose to see it as an opportunity to practice resilience or to develop a new skill. For example, if we lose a job, instead of succumbing to despair, we can view it as an opportunity to explore new paths or to reflect on what truly matters to us. By changing our perspective, we reclaim our power over our emotions, allowing us to approach life's challenges with courage rather than fear.

Epictetus saw reframing as a way to exercise control over our thoughts, the one area that is always within our reach. This technique is not about denying the pain or difficulty of a situation but about choosing to see it in a light that empowers us. By reframing negative events, we learn to view life as a series of lessons, each moment an opportunity to grow in wisdom and strength. This mindset shift can be profoundly liberating, allowing us to face adversity with a sense of purpose and confidence.

Practicing Acceptance: The Stoic Path to Peace

For Epictetus, acceptance was not a passive resignation but an active choice to align oneself with reality. He taught that by accepting what we cannot change, we free ourselves from the frustration and bitterness that come from wishing life were different. Acceptance is not giving up; it is a decision to find peace in the present, to live fully in the moment without being weighed down by regret or longing.

The practice of acceptance is particularly relevant in today's world, where we are constantly pressured to pursue perfection, to achieve, to control every aspect of our lives. But Stoicism teaches that true peace comes not from the pursuit of control but from the ability to accept things as they are. By practicing acceptance, we release the need to fight against reality, allowing us to move through life with greater ease and tranquility.

Epictetus believed that acceptance was a skill, one that could be cultivated through reflection and discipline. When faced with a challenge, he would remind himself to accept what was beyond his influence and focus on what he could control—his response, his thoughts, and his actions. This approach allowed him to face even the most difficult circumstances with a sense of calm, knowing that his peace did not depend on changing the world but on changing himself.

Building Inner Strength Through Self-Mastery

The dichotomy of control teaches that our true strength lies not in dominating others or bending the world to our will, but in mastering ourselves. Epictetus saw self-mastery as the highest form of freedom, a state of being in which we are unshaken by external events because our peace is rooted within. By focusing on our own thoughts, choices, and actions, we cultivate a resilience that cannot be taken from us.

Self-mastery requires discipline and mindfulness, a commitment to examine our thoughts and to choose responses that reflect our values. When we learn to control our inner world, we become less reactive, less driven by fear, anger, or desire. We develop a calm strength, an ability to remain centered in the face of life's storms. For Epictetus, this inner strength was the essence of Stoic wisdom, a path to a life of purpose and fulfillment.

An Exercise in Applying the Dichotomy of Control

To make Epictetus' teaching on control practical, consider this exercise:

Identify a Current Challenge: Think about a situation in your life that is causing you stress or frustration. Write it down, describing it as clearly as possible.

Determine What You Can Control: Break down the situation into parts, identifying which aspects are within your control and which are not. Focus on the specific actions, thoughts, or responses that are yours to command.

Release What You Cannot Control: Consciously choose to let go of any elements that are beyond your influence. Remind yourself that your peace depends not on controlling the outcome but on controlling your response.

Take Action on What You Can Control: Commit to taking action in the areas within your power, focusing on what you can do to respond with integrity, patience, or resilience.

Reflect on the Outcome: After you have taken action, observe the outcome without attachment, reminding yourself that your well-being does not depend on external results but on your own peace of mind.

This exercise can be repeated in any situation, offering a structured way to apply the dichotomy of control to everyday challenges. By practicing this approach, we train ourselves to focus on what truly matters, to engage with life on our own terms, and to find peace regardless of how events unfold.

Finding Freedom Within the Boundaries of Control

Epictetus' teaching on the dichotomy of control is not just a tool for managing stress; it is a philosophy of life, a path to freedom that remains accessible to everyone, regardless of circumstance. By focusing on what lies within our control, we cultivate a strength that no hardship can diminish and a peace that no external force can shatter. We discover that our happiness and fulfillment are not determined by what happens to us but by how we choose to respond.

In a world filled with uncertainty and change, Epictetus' wisdom offers a refuge, a reminder that while we may not control the storms of life, we can control how we navigate them. This teaching, simple yet profound, remains as relevant today as it was in ancient times, a testament to the enduring power of Stoic philosophy.

Through the dichotomy of control, we find a way to live with purpose, resilience, and peace. We learn that true freedom is not the ability to control the world, but the ability to control ourselves. And in that mastery, we discover a strength that is unbreakable, a freedom that is timeless, and a peace that endures beyond the reach of fate.

Chapter 6

Conquering Overthinking & Anxiety

Epictetus once said, "Men are disturbed not by things, but by the views they take of them." This simple insight holds a profound key to understanding the root of much of our anxiety and overthinking. In Epictetus' view, our suffering is not necessarily caused by external events, but by our judgments and interpretations of those events. It is the mental stories we create, the meaning we assign to situations, that often turns a minor issue into a source of anxiety. Epictetus believed that while we cannot always control what happens around us, we can control how we think about it. By becoming mindful of our judgments, we can transform our relationship with anxiety, reducing our tendency to overthink and find greater peace of mind.

In today's fast-paced world, overthinking has become almost a cultural epidemic.

We worry about the future, replay conversations in our heads, and second-guess our decisions. Anxiety often stems not from the events themselves, but from the endless cycle of thoughts and judgments we build around them. Epictetus' teachings on judgment offer us a way out of this cycle, showing us that we have the power to reinterpret and reframe our experiences. This chapter explores how to use Stoic insights to re-evaluate our thoughts, challenge our initial reactions, and cultivate a calm, balanced mind.

The Role of Judgment in Anxiety

Anxiety, at its core, is often a response to uncertainty, a reaction to situations where we fear a negative outcome. But Epictetus saw that it is not the uncertainty itself that causes us distress—it is our interpretation of it. When we encounter an uncertain or challenging situation, our mind quickly fills in the gaps with assumptions, judgments, and expectations. We imagine worst-case scenarios, anticipate failure, or dwell on negative possibilities. This process, left unchecked, leads to overthinking, a mental state where we become consumed by thoughts and worries that have little grounding in reality.

Epictetus taught that much of our anxiety could be alleviated by understanding that our initial judgment is just one possible interpretation, not an absolute truth. He encouraged his students to become aware of their judgments and to question whether they were helping or harming them. By challenging our automatic reactions, we can learn to approach situations with a clearer perspective, reducing the mental clutter that feeds anxiety.

Consider, for example, the common fear of public speaking. For many people, the thought of speaking in front of a crowd triggers anxiety. They imagine that they'll forget their words, be judged, or embarrass themselves. But Epictetus would ask us to examine these assumptions. Is it certain that we'll forget our words? Is it guaranteed that others will judge us? Or is it possible that these fears are simply judgments, stories we've told ourselves that have little basis in reality? By questioning our interpretations, we can begin to see that much of our anxiety is a product of our own minds, a self-imposed barrier that we have the power to dismantle.

Re-Evaluating Thoughts: A Stoic Practice

One of the most effective ways to apply Epictetus' teachings on judgment is through the practice of re-evaluation—an exercise that involves examining our thoughts and challenging initial judgments that may be causing unnecessary anxiety. This technique allows us to break the cycle of overthinking by consciously choosing to see situations in a more balanced light. Here's a step-by-step guide to re-evaluation:

1.   Identify the Thought: Start by noticing the thought that is causing you distress or anxiety. It might be a worry about the future, a fear of failure, or a negative assumption about a situation. Write it down, describing it as clearly as possible.

2.   Examine the Judgment: Look at the thought and ask yourself if it is based on objective fact or subjective interpretation. Is there evidence to support this judgment, or is it an assumption? For example, if your thought is, "I will fail at this task," ask yourself if there is concrete evidence that failure is inevitable, or if this is simply a fear.

3.   Challenge the Thought: Actively question the validity of the thought. Consider alternative explanations or perspectives. Could the outcome be different from what you fear? Is there another way to view the situation that would

reduce your anxiety? By opening yourself to other possibilities, you lessen the power of your initial judgment.

4.   Replace the Thought with a Balanced Perspective: After examining and challenging the thought, replace it with a balanced, realistic statement. Instead of "I will fail at this task," you might say, "I will do my best with the resources I have, and that is enough." This shift in perspective allows you to focus on what you can control while releasing unnecessary worry.

5.   Practice Acceptance: Finally, accept that uncertainty is a natural part of life. Acknowledge that while you cannot predict the future, you can choose to face it with resilience and calm. Epictetus reminds us that peace comes not from eliminating uncertainty, but from accepting it and focusing on our own responses.

A Case Study in Reframing: Sarah's Story

To illustrate the power of re-evaluating thoughts, let's consider the example of Sarah, a marketing professional who found herself constantly anxious about her job performance. Every time her boss gave her feedback, she would assume the worst, interpreting every comment as a sign of dissatisfaction. Her mind would race with thoughts like, "I'm not good enough," "I'll never succeed in this role," and "I'm probably going to be fired." Over time, this pattern of thinking became exhausting, fueling her anxiety and undermining her confidence.

One day, Sarah decided to apply the Stoic practice of re-evaluation. She began by writing down her initial thoughts after a performance review. Her thoughts included assumptions like, "My boss is disappointed in me," and "I'll never be able to meet his expectations." She then examined each thought, asking herself if it was based on fact or judgment. Was there any clear evidence that her boss was dissatisfied, or was this her own fear projecting onto the situation?

As she questioned her assumptions, Sarah realized that much of her anxiety stemmed from her own self-doubt rather than any specific feedback. She decided to replace her initial thoughts with a more balanced perspective: "My boss gave me constructive feedback, and this is an opportunity to grow." By shifting her focus from her fear of failure to her potential for improvement, Sarah was able to reduce her anxiety and approach her work with renewed confidence.

> *Epictetus believed that by developing a sense of detachment, we can create space between ourselves and our mental reactions, reducing their hold over us.*

This example demonstrates how re-evaluating thoughts can help us dismantle the narratives that fuel anxiety. When we learn to view situations from a place of calm and objectivity, we break free from the cycle of overthinking, allowing us to engage with life in a more relaxed, open-minded way.

The Art of Practicing Detachment

Another powerful Stoic technique for conquering overthinking is the practice of detachment—a process of mentally stepping back from our thoughts and observing them without judgment. Epictetus believed that by developing a sense of detachment, we can create space between ourselves and our mental reactions, reducing their hold over us. Detachment does not mean ignoring or suppressing thoughts; rather, it involves acknowledging them without becoming entangled in them.

To practice detachment, imagine your mind as a river, with thoughts flowing by like leaves on the surface. Instead of reaching out and clinging to each leaf, simply watch them float past, observing them without judgment or attachment. When an anxious thought arises, notice it, but resist the urge to engage with it. Allow it to drift away, knowing that it does not define you.

This exercise can be especially helpful when dealing with repetitive worries or fears that seem difficult to shake. By practicing detachment, you train your mind to observe thoughts without reacting to them, creating a calm space from which you can choose your response. Over time, detachment allows you to approach life's challenges with greater clarity, free from the constant chatter of anxious thoughts.

Turning Anxiety into Purpose

One of Epictetus' most radical teachings was his belief that challenges and difficulties can be transformed into opportunities for growth. He saw anxiety not as an enemy to be defeated but as a teacher, a force that could help us refine our inner strength. By viewing anxiety as a signal rather than a threat, we can learn to approach it with curiosity and resilience, asking ourselves what lessons it may hold.

For example, if you feel anxious about a presentation, rather than viewing this anxiety as a failure or weakness, consider it a sign that the presentation is important to you. Use this awareness to prepare more effectively, to refine your message, and to practice with intention. By transforming anxiety into purposeful action, you shift the focus from fear to empowerment, using the energy of anxiety to propel you toward your goals.

Epictetus believed that each moment of discomfort was an opportunity to practice virtue, to strengthen our commitment to resilience and self-mastery. Instead of fearing anxiety, we can view it as a chance to exercise patience, courage, and determination. This mindset shift transforms our relationship with anxiety, allowing us to approach life's challenges with a sense of purpose and calm.

An Exercise in Challenging Overthinking

To make Epictetus' teachings on judgment practical, consider this exercise:

1.   Identify a Source of Overthinking: Think of a situation that often triggers overthinking or anxiety for you. Describe it in detail, noting the specific thoughts that come to mind.

2.   Question the Validity of Each Thought: For each thought, ask yourself if it is based on fact or assumption. Are you jumping to conclusions or creating unnecessary worries? Write down alternative ways to view the situation.

3.   Replace the Thought with a Balanced Statement: After challenging each thought, replace it with a balanced, realistic statement that acknowledges uncertainty without succumbing to fear.

4.   Visualize a Calm Response: Imagine yourself facing the situation with a calm mind, responding from a place of clarity and control. Visualize yourself remaining composed, accepting the outcome without judgment.

5.   Practice Detachment Daily: Commit to practicing detachment by observing your thoughts each day, allowing

them to pass without judgment. Notice when you begin to overthink, and remind yourself that your peace of mind depends on your ability to let go.

Finding Freedom in Perspective

Epictetus' teachings on judgment offer a way to free ourselves from the prison of overthinking. By recognizing that our anxiety often stems from our own interpretations, we gain the power to change our relationship with our thoughts. We learn that peace is not a matter of eliminating challenges but of transforming how we view them. Through the practices of re-evaluation, detachment, and purposeful action, we build a mindset that is resilient, adaptable, and calm.

In the end, conquering overthinking is not about controlling every thought but about choosing which thoughts to engage with and which to release. Epictetus reminds us that while we cannot control the world, we can control our minds—and in that choice lies a profound freedom, a path to a life lived with purpose, clarity, and tranquility. Through his wisdom, we discover that true peace is not the absence of anxiety, but the ability to rise above it, to engage with life fully, and to find meaning in every moment, no matter how uncertain.

"The universe is change; our life is what our thoughts make it."

—Marcus Aurelius

Chapter 7

Building Resilience in a Divisive World

Epictetus lived in a world filled with unrest, where political turmoil, social hierarchies, and external pressures shaped everyday life. Yet, despite these chaotic surroundings, he found a way to maintain his inner peace and fortify his spirit against the currents of conflict that surrounded him. His philosophy did not rely on the hope that external conditions would change but rather on the conviction that one's inner life could remain untouched by external circumstances. In our modern world, divided by political ideologies, social conflicts, and the pressures of a constantly connected society, Epictetus' teachings on resilience offer a powerful guide for cultivating strength, calm, and clarity within ourselves, regardless of the external chaos. This chapter explores how to apply Epictetus' principles to build resilience in a world that often feels fractured, helping us to remain grounded, balanced, and unshaken by the divisions around us.

The Foundation of Resilience:

Detachment from Others' Opinions Epictetus was acutely aware of the human tendency to seek approval from others, a habit that often leads to inner turmoil and a loss of autonomy. He taught that true resilience begins when we detach ourselves from the need for external validation, recognizing that our worth does not depend on others' opinions or judgments. Epictetus reminded his students that people's judgments are beyond our control; we cannot dictate their thoughts or reactions. To base our peace on something as uncontrollable as others' opinions is to hand over our power, to make ourselves vulnerable to every whim and perception that others may hold. He urged his students to focus on their own actions, to live in accordance with their own principles, and to find satisfaction in their integrity rather than in approval. In practice, this means choosing to value our own actions and choices over how others perceive them.

When faced with criticism or praise, Epictetus would encourage us to ask: "Did I act with integrity? Did I remain true to my values?" If the answer is yes, then we can remain at peace, knowing that our sense of self is rooted in our own principles. This perspective is especially valuable in a divisive world where opinions are frequently polarizing. By detaching from others' judgments, we build resilience against the social pressures that so often dictate our actions, allowing us to navigate life with a calm and unwavering sense of purpose.

Focusing on Virtue Over Victory In a society that often celebrates victory and dominance, Epictetus taught that virtue—living in alignment with one's principles—is the true mark of success. He believed that resilience is built not by striving to "win" every conflict or to assert our views over others, but by holding steadfast to values like kindness, honesty, and patience, even when they are tested by others' actions.

This approach transforms how we engage with divisive issues, shifting our focus from the need to be "right" or to convince others to a commitment to act with virtue in every situation. For Epictetus, resilience came from an internal sense of purpose that was not swayed by the changing tides of public opinion or personal conflicts. He would advise us to ask ourselves, "Am I living in accordance with my values?" rather than "Have I convinced others to agree with me?" This shift in perspective allows us to approach disagreements with a spirit of humility and openness rather than defensiveness.

It enables us to engage in conversations without becoming consumed by the need to dominate or convert others to our perspective. This resilience, rooted in virtue rather than victory, allows us to participate in a world of opposing views without losing our sense of self or peace.

The Practice of Emotional Detachment

Epictetus taught that building resilience requires emotional detachment from external events. This does not mean ignoring our emotions or becoming indifferent to the world around us; rather, it involves cultivating a balanced perspective that allows us to remain unaffected by the emotional highs and lows of life. Epictetus believed that emotional detachment begins by recognizing that while we may experience feelings of anger, fear, or frustration, we do not have to be ruled by them. These emotions are natural responses, but it is our choice whether we allow them to control our actions. He encouraged his students to observe their emotions with a sense of distance, to acknowledge them without immediately reacting. This practice of emotional detachment is especially valuable in today's world, where we are constantly exposed to news, opinions, and events that can easily trigger strong reactions.

When we cultivate emotional detachment, we create a buffer between ourselves and the external world, allowing us to approach situations with a calm and measured response. By practicing emotional detachment, we strengthen our ability to engage with life's challenges without being swept away by them, enabling us to face conflicts and pressures with resilience and clarity.

Setting Boundaries: Protecting Inner Peace

One of the key aspects of building resilience is learning to set boundaries, both with others and with the information we consume. Epictetus understood that our peace is often compromised when we allow external forces to intrude on our inner life. He taught that setting boundaries is an act of self-respect, a way of safeguarding our mental space from unnecessary disruptions. In our connected world, where we are constantly bombarded with information and opinions, setting boundaries is essential for maintaining resilience. This might mean limiting exposure to social media, choosing not to engage in certain conversations, or being selective about the company we keep. By setting boundaries, we protect our inner peace, ensuring that we have the mental clarity to face life's challenges without becoming overwhelmed. Epictetus would encourage us to be mindful of the influences we allow into our lives, recognizing that resilience requires a commitment to prioritize our peace over the demands of others. When we set boundaries, we create a safe space within ourselves, a place of calm that remains untouched by the chaos outside.

An Exercise in Building Resilience Through Stoic Reflection

To make Epictetus' teachings on resilience practical, consider this exercise: 1.

Identify a Source of Conflict: Think of a situation or relationship in your life that causes stress or tension. Write it down, describing the specific elements that challenge your peace.

2. **Examine Your Reactions**: Reflect on your usual response to this conflict. Do you feel the need to control others' opinions, to prove a point, or to win the argument? Write down these reactions and consider how they may be contributing to your stress.

3. **Apply the Dichotomy of Control**: Ask yourself which aspects of this situation are within your control and which are not. Focus on what you can control—your own actions, words, and perspective—and release any attachment to controlling others.

4. **Set an Intention of Virtue**: Choose a virtue you want to embody in this situation, such as patience, kindness, or honesty. Write down how you can act from this virtue regardless of how others respond.

5. **Commit to Emotional Detachment**: Remind yourself to observe your emotions without being ruled by them. Practice responding calmly rather than reacting impulsively, knowing that your peace depends on your choices, not the actions of others.

A Case Study in Resilience: John's Story To illustrate the application of these principles, let's consider the story of John, a school teacher who struggled with the divisive political discussions that often took place in his staff room.

John was passionate about his views, but he found that engaging in these conversations left him feeling frustrated and anxious. He often felt compelled to argue his point, to convince others that his perspective was valid. Over time, this need to assert his views began to take a toll on his mental well-being. Inspired by Epictetus' teachings, John decided to apply the Stoic approach to resilience. He began by setting an intention to focus on virtue rather than victory. Instead of trying to convince others, he chose to embody patience and respect, recognizing that his peace did not depend on whether others agreed with him. He also practiced emotional detachment, reminding himself that while he cared about the issues, he did not have to become emotionally entangled in every discussion. By focusing on his own behavior and releasing the need to control others, John found that he was able to engage in conversations without feeling stressed or defensive. He created an inner boundary, a space of calm that allowed him to listen without losing his peace.

This experience taught him that resilience is not about changing others but about remaining true to one's values, a lesson that transformed his approach to conflict and strengthened his sense of self.

Resilience as a Daily Practice Epictetus saw resilience not as a trait one is born with but as a skill that can be cultivated through daily practice. He believed that resilience grows from small acts of patience, self-control, and acceptance, each one building upon the last to create a foundation of inner strength.

This means that every moment of frustration, every disagreement, every challenge is an opportunity to strengthen our resilience. By approaching each day with the intention to live in accordance with our principles, we develop a resilience that becomes unshakable, a calm that remains steady even in the face of conflict.

The Power of Perspective: Viewing Conflict as a Teacher

Epictetus also encouraged his students to view conflict and challenges as opportunities for growth. Rather than seeing adversity as a setback, he taught that each difficulty was a chance to practice patience, humility, and self-control. By reframing challenges in this way, we can transform how we experience them, viewing them not as sources of stress but as teachers that help us build resilience. This perspective allows us to face life's challenges with a sense of purpose, knowing that each test of our patience is an opportunity to strengthen our character.

Finding Peace in a Divisive World

Epictetus' teachings on resilience offer a path to peace that is both practical and timeless. By focusing on our own actions, embodying virtue, and detaching from others' judgments, we cultivate a resilience that allows us to navigate life's conflicts with calm and clarity. In a world that often feels fragmented and contentious, this inner peace becomes a refuge, a place where we can rest, recharge, and remain true to ourselves. Through Epictetus' wisdom, we discover that resilience is not about escaping conflict but about facing it with a heart that is steady and a mind that is clear.

We learn that true strength lies not in dominating others but in mastering ourselves, in holding fast to our values even when the world around us is divided. This resilience, rooted in self-mastery, is the foundation of a peaceful life, a life where we are free from the need to control others, unshaken by external judgments, and at peace within ourselves. By embracing Epictetus' teachings, we find that we have the power to live with integrity, to face life's challenges with courage, and to build a world of resilience and calm from within.

Chapter 8

Living a Life of Integrity and Virtue

For Epictetus, living with integrity and virtue was not just a moral aspiration but the essence of a life well-lived. In his teachings, integrity was the very foundation upon which resilience and inner peace were built. He believed that to live with integrity is to align our actions, thoughts, and intentions with our highest principles, creating a life that is both resilient and rooted in authenticity. This emphasis on virtue and integrity forms the heart of Stoic philosophy, guiding us to approach life's challenges with consistency, clarity, and a commitment to our true selves.

Epictetus saw virtue as the one constant in a world of change and unpredictability, a compass that grounds us when external circumstances try to pull us off course. This chapter explores the journey of cultivating a life of integrity and virtue according to Epictetus' teachings, and it provides readers with practical exercises for making these principles a living, breathing reality.

Integrity, in the Stoic sense, begins with self-awareness. Epictetus believed that before we can live in alignment with our values, we must first understand what we truly value. This requires a process of introspection, a willingness to look within ourselves and question our motives, desires, and intentions. Epictetus often advised his students to take time to reflect on what they stood for, urging them to define their personal principles rather than allowing societal pressures or external influences to dictate their beliefs. To know oneself, he taught, is to lay the foundation for a life that cannot be easily swayed by temporary pleasures or fleeting rewards. Integrity is a way of standing firm, rooted in a sense of purpose that transcends external validation or superficial gains.

For many of us, the journey toward self-awareness can be daunting. It requires us to confront uncomfortable truths about our strengths and weaknesses, to acknowledge areas where we may fall short of our own ideals. Yet Epictetus saw this honest self-examination as an essential step toward living a virtuous life. By identifying our values—such as honesty, compassion, courage, or humility—we create a moral compass that guides our actions and decisions, ensuring that our lives are marked by consistency and alignment between what we believe and how we behave.

This process of clarifying our values is not a one-time event but an ongoing practice, a continual refinement of our understanding of what it means to live with integrity in each stage of life.

Epictetus also taught that living with integrity requires the courage to act in accordance with our values, even when doing so may be challenging. He believed that integrity is not demonstrated in moments of ease or convenience but in times of trial when we are tempted to compromise our principles for personal gain or to conform to social pressures.

For Epictetus, resilience in the face of these challenges is the true mark of a person committed to virtue, someone who values their character above temporary benefits or the approval of others. He often reminded his students that virtue is not something we claim with words but something we prove through action. To live with integrity means to choose what is right over what is easy, to act in alignment with our values even when it is inconvenient or difficult. This unwavering commitment to virtue builds a resilience that is unbreakable, a strength that allows us to face adversity with dignity and purpose.

One of the essential components of integrity, according to Epictetus, is accountability. He taught that to live a life of virtue, we must hold ourselves accountable for our actions, to examine our behavior with honesty and humility. Accountability, as

Epictetus saw it, is not about judging ourselves harshly or dwelling on our mistakes, but rather learning from them and using each misstep as an opportunity to grow in virtue. Epictetus believed that accountability is a daily practice, a habit of self-reflection that strengthens our trust in ourselves and deepens our commitment to our principles. By holding ourselves accountable, we cultivate a sense of self-respect and self-trust, knowing that our actions are guided by our values rather than by fleeting impulses or external influences.

To make Epictetus' teachings on integrity practical, consider incorporating a daily reflection exercise into your routine. At the end of each day, take a few minutes to review your actions and choices, asking yourself if they were aligned with your values. Identify any moments where you may have compromised your integrity, and consider how you might approach similar situations in the future with a greater commitment to your principles. By making this reflection a regular practice, you strengthen your resolve to live with integrity, creating a life that is consistent, honorable, and resilient.

Epictetus believed that integrity is also sustained by a commitment to truth, to seeing ourselves and the world as they are rather than as we wish them to be. He taught that wisdom begins with a clear perception of reality, a willingness to confront uncomfortable truths rather than to ignore or deny them. For Epictetus, living with integrity means embracing honesty, acknowledging our limitations and areas for growth, and striving to improve ourselves without falling into the traps of illusion or pretense.

This commitment to truth builds a life that is genuine and grounded, a life based on reality rather than on the false comforts of denial or self-deception.

Another vital aspect of Epictetus' teaching on integrity is the importance of humility. He believed that humility is not only a virtue in itself but also a foundation for living with integrity. By approaching life with humility, we recognize that we are always in the process of learning and growing, that our understanding of virtue and integrity is constantly evolving.

Epictetus taught that humility allows us to remain open to feedback, to be willing to admit when we are wrong, and to seek out opportunities for self-improvement. He believed that humility is what allows us to hold ourselves accountable without becoming consumed by pride or shame, to strive for virtue while remaining grounded in the reality of our imperfections.

Epictetus also emphasized that integrity involves consistency—a commitment to live in alignment with our values not only in public but also in private. He taught that true integrity is not about impressing others or seeking validation; it is about living honestly with ourselves, ensuring that our actions reflect our principles even when no one is watching.

This consistency builds self-trust, a sense of inner confidence that comes from knowing that we are true to ourselves. By practicing integrity in all areas of our lives, we create a sense of wholeness, a life that is aligned with our values at every level. This consistency strengthens our resilience, allowing us to face external pressures and challenges without compromising our principles.

In his teachings, Epictetus often reminded his students that integrity and virtue are not destinations to be reached but practices to be lived. He saw the pursuit of virtue as a lifelong journey, one that requires ongoing commitment and effort. Epictetus believed that each day offers an opportunity to strengthen our commitment to integrity, to choose actions that reflect our values, and to grow in wisdom and character.

He taught that by approaching life with this mindset, we create a resilience that is unbreakable, a strength that comes from knowing that our happiness and fulfillment are not dependent on external circumstances but on our own dedication to living a life of virtue.

To embody Epictetus' teachings on integrity and virtue, consider integrating the following practices into your life:

Define Your Values: Take time to reflect on the values that are most important to you, such as honesty, compassion, courage, or humility. Write them down, and use them as a guide for your actions and decisions.

Daily Reflection: At the end of each day, review your actions and choices, asking yourself if they were aligned with your values. Identify any moments where you may have compromised your integrity, and consider how you can approach similar situations in the future with greater alignment to your principles.

Practice Humility: Approach life with an open mind, recognizing that you are always learning and growing. Be willing to admit when you are wrong, to seek feedback, and to view each experience as an opportunity for self-improvement.

Consistency in Action: Strive to live in alignment with your values in all areas of your life, both in public and in private. Ensure that your actions reflect your principles even when no one is watching, creating a sense of wholeness and self-trust.

Accountability Partner: Consider finding someone you trust who shares your commitment to living with integrity. Set up regular check-ins to discuss your progress, to share any challenges you may be facing, and to hold each other accountable for staying true to your values.

By incorporating these practices into our lives, we take steps to build a life of integrity and virtue, a life that reflects our highest principles in each action and decision. Epictetus' teachings remind us that true strength and resilience come from within, from our commitment to living a life of purpose and authenticity.

Through the practice of integrity, we create a foundation of peace and strength, a foundation that allows us to face life's challenges with courage, clarity, and a deep sense of self-respect.

In the end, Epictetus saw integrity and virtue as the foundation of a life that is both meaningful and fulfilling. He believed that by aligning our actions with our values, we build a resilience that is unshaken by external circumstances, a peace that comes from knowing that we are true to ourselves. Through his teachings, we learn that integrity is not a single achievement but a daily commitment, a journey of self-discovery, growth, and dedication to our highest principles.

By cultivating a life of virtue, we build a resilience that is unbreakable, a strength that endures through all of life's challenges, and a peace that remains constant, grounded in the knowledge that we have lived with honesty, courage, and purpose.

This resilience, rooted in integrity, is the essence of a life well-lived, a life that reflects the wisdom, strength, and depth of character that Epictetus believed was the highest form of human achievement.

"Nothing is at last sacred but the integrity of your
own mind."

—Marcus Aurelius

Chapter 9

Practical Stoicism

Real-Life Applications

Epictetus' philosophy is often celebrated for its depth and insight, but its true power lies in its practical application. To him, philosophy was not an abstract discipline meant only for scholars; it was a way of living, a set of tools designed to help us navigate life's challenges with clarity, resilience, and purpose. Epictetus believed that the principles of Stoicism should be applied to daily life, allowing us to cultivate peace, strength, and wisdom regardless of external circumstances.

Stoicism, as he taught it, is a philosophy of action, one that invites us to practice its teachings through conscious engagement with the world around us. In this chapter, we delve into the practical applications of Stoicism, offering exercises, tools, and real-life examples inspired by Epictetus' teachings to help readers integrate Stoic principles into their own lives.

One of the foundational applications of Stoicism is the practice of mindfulness. Epictetus taught that mindfulness—or the ability to be fully present and aware of our thoughts and actions—is the cornerstone of self-control. He believed that by paying attention to our thoughts as they arise, we can observe our mental reactions without becoming entangled in them. This practice allows us to see our emotions and impulses for what they are—temporary states rather than absolute truths. For Epictetus, mindfulness was a means of cultivating detachment from negative emotions, a way of separating ourselves from the noise of reactive thinking so that we can approach each moment with clarity and intention.

Mindfulness, as Epictetus understood it, requires us to observe our thoughts without judgment. When we become aware of a feeling of anger, anxiety, or frustration, instead of reacting impulsively, we pause and consider whether our response is aligned with our values. By observing our thoughts and feelings with a sense of distance, we create space for choice, a gap between stimulus and response. In practical terms, this might mean noticing the rise of anger in a difficult conversation and choosing to respond calmly rather than letting our emotions take control. Through mindfulness, we learn to live with greater awareness, to respond rather than react, and to cultivate a sense of peace that is grounded in our own conscious choices rather than in external events.

Another powerful Stoic practice is reframing—a technique that involves changing the way we interpret situations to reduce stress and increase resilience. Epictetus believed that much of our suffering comes not from the events themselves but from our interpretation of them. He taught that by reframing our perspective, by choosing to see challenges as opportunities for growth or as tests of our character, we can transform our relationship with adversity.

For example, if we face a setback at work, instead of viewing it as a failure, we might choose to see it as an opportunity to refine our skills and strengthen our resolve. By reframing challenges in this way, we shift our focus from what we cannot control to what we can—our own actions, our attitude, and our ability to adapt. Reframing is a practical tool that empowers us to approach life with a mindset of resilience and openness, allowing us to see difficulties not as obstacles but as stepping stones toward personal growth.

Incorporating reframing into daily life begins with a simple question: "What can I learn from this?" By asking this question, we open ourselves to new possibilities, to insights that might otherwise be hidden beneath our initial reactions. For instance, if we experience disappointment or frustration, we can pause and consider how this moment might be teaching us patience, humility, or perseverance.

Reframing is not about denying the reality of our challenges but about choosing to see them through a lens that empowers us. This shift in perspective enables us to face life's difficulties with a sense of purpose, knowing that each experience, no matter how challenging, contributes to our growth.

Stoicism also offers practical techniques for managing difficult emotions, such as anger, fear, and sadness. Epictetus taught that while these emotions are natural, we do not have to be ruled by them. He believed that by developing emotional detachment—by observing our emotions without identifying with them—we can reduce their power over us. In practice, this means learning to step back when we feel strong emotions, to observe the sensations in our body and the thoughts in our mind without reacting to them.

By practicing emotional detachment, we create a space where we can choose our response, allowing us to handle difficult situations with a calm and measured approach. This technique is especially valuable in moments of conflict or stress, where strong emotions can often cloud our judgment and lead to impulsive actions.

To cultivate emotional detachment, consider the following exercise: the next time you feel a strong emotion, take a moment to pause and simply observe it. Notice how the emotion feels in your body, the thoughts it brings up, and the impulse to react. Instead of acting on the impulse, take a few deep breaths and allow the emotion to pass. Remind yourself that this feeling is temporary, that it does not define you. By practicing this approach regularly, you develop the skill of emotional detachment, a resilience that enables you to face life's challenges with calm and clarity.

Epictetus also encouraged his students to practice gratitude as a means of cultivating inner peace and resilience. He believed that by focusing on what we have rather than on what we lack, we can reduce feelings of dissatisfaction and develop a sense of contentment that is unshaken by external circumstances. In

practical terms, this means taking time each day to reflect on the things we are grateful for, whether it be our health, our relationships, or simply the beauty of a moment. By practicing gratitude, we shift our focus from scarcity to abundance, from lack to appreciation, creating a mindset that is more resilient to the ups and downs of life.

To make Epictetus' teachings practical in everyday life, consider incorporating the following gratitude exercise: each evening, take a few moments to write down three things you are grateful for from that day. These can be big or small—a conversation with a friend, a moment of quiet, or an accomplishment at work. Reflect on how these experiences contribute to your well-being, allowing yourself to feel a sense of appreciation for each one.

Over time, this practice of gratitude becomes a habit, a lens through which you view life with greater resilience and joy.

Another valuable Stoic exercise is the practice of premeditatio malorum, or "pre-meditation of evils." This technique involves mentally preparing for potential challenges by imagining various difficulties we might face and rehearsing how we would respond. Epictetus taught that by considering potential setbacks in advance, we can reduce the shock and disappointment that often accompany unexpected challenges. This exercise is not about dwelling on negative possibilities but about cultivating a realistic mindset, one that accepts the unpredictability of life and prepares for it with calm and resilience.

To practice premeditatio malorum, think of a situation you are likely to face in the coming days—an important meeting, a family gathering, or a challenging project. Consider what could go wrong, not to create anxiety, but to prepare yourself for a calm and effective response. Imagine yourself facing these challenges with patience, resilience, and integrity.

Visualize how you would act in alignment with your values, regardless of the outcome. By rehearsing these scenarios, you build a mental resilience that allows you to face real-life challenges with greater composure and confidence.

One of the most profound insights of Epictetus' teachings is the recognition that our peace and fulfillment are not determined by external circumstances but by our own choices and actions. He believed that the pursuit of virtue—living in alignment with our highest values—is the ultimate source of resilience and inner peace.

By focusing on our own actions, by choosing responses that reflect our principles, we cultivate a sense of purpose and integrity that strengthens us in the face of adversity.

To bring this concept into daily life, consider setting a personal intention for virtue each morning. Choose a quality you want to embody that day—patience, kindness, honesty, or courage— and make a commitment to act in accordance with that quality, regardless of the challenges you may face. Throughout the day, return to this intention, using it as a guide for your actions and responses. By grounding yourself in your values, you build a resilience that is unshaken by external events, a sense of purpose that guides you through each moment with clarity and strength.

Epictetus' teachings remind us that the power to shape our lives lies not in controlling the world around us but in controlling how we respond to it. Through practical Stoicism, we gain the tools to navigate life's challenges with grace, to cultivate resilience and inner peace, and to live with a sense of purpose and integrity.

By applying these techniques—mindfulness, reframing, emotional detachment, gratitude, premeditatio malorum, and intentional virtue—we create a life that is both fulfilling and resilient, a life that reflects the depth and wisdom of Stoic philosophy.

In the end, Epictetus' philosophy is a call to action, an invitation to live each day with intention, awareness, and commitment to our highest values. Through the practical application of Stoicism, we discover that true peace and fulfillment are not gifts from the world but gifts we give ourselves by choosing to live with integrity, courage, and gratitude.

By embracing this way of life, we find that we have the strength to face whatever challenges come our way, the resilience to grow through adversity, and the wisdom to live each moment with purpose and clarity.

"To live happily is an inward power of the soul."

—Marcus Aurelius

Chapter 10

The Timeless Wisdom of Epictetus

As the centuries have passed, countless philosophies, ideologies, and theories have come and gone, each leaving its mark on history. Yet, some teachings endure, standing the test of time and offering wisdom as relevant today as it was in ages past. Among these timeless philosophies is that of Epictetus, a former slave turned philosopher whose insights into resilience, integrity, and self-mastery continue to speak to readers worldwide. Epictetus' wisdom is timeless because it speaks to the core of the human experience. He understood that while circumstances may change, the inner struggles we face—the quest for peace, the desire for purpose, the longing for resilience—are as old as humanity itself. In this final chapter, we explore the enduring relevance of Epictetus' teachings, showing how they provide a roadmap for achieving inner peace, emotional strength, and a life of purpose.

Epictetus believed that true freedom lies not in external circumstances but in mastering our own minds. He saw that life is inherently unpredictable, filled with events beyond our control. Yet, instead of viewing this reality with despair, he embraced it, teaching that our inner freedom is grounded in how we respond to life's challenges. This perspective is what makes Epictetus' philosophy so powerful; it gives us a sense of agency, reminding us that we are not merely passive participants in life but active shapers of our experience. By focusing on what lies within our control—our own thoughts, judgments, and actions—we gain the power to live with purpose and resilience, regardless of what the world throws our way.

Epictetus' approach to freedom through self-mastery is especially relevant in today's world, where many of us feel overwhelmed by the pressures of modern life. We live in an age of constant stimulation, with news, social media, and external demands bombarding us from every direction.

This perpetual noise can make it difficult to connect with our inner selves, to find the clarity and peace we crave. Epictetus reminds us that the key to inner peace lies not in escaping from the world but in changing our relationship with it. By cultivating self-mastery, by learning to direct our thoughts and actions with intention, we create a calm and resilient mind that remains steady even amidst the chaos of life.

One of the most powerful aspects of Epictetus' wisdom is his teaching on acceptance—a concept that resonates deeply in a world often defined by resistance and control. Epictetus taught that while we cannot change many of life's events, we can choose how we respond to them. Acceptance, as he saw it, is not about resignation but about embracing reality as it is, freeing ourselves from the constant need to resist what we cannot change. This acceptance is a source of liberation, a way of finding peace in every moment by choosing to align our will with the nature of reality itself.

To illustrate the power of acceptance, consider the story of Marcus, a modern reader who discovered Stoic philosophy during a difficult time. Marcus had always been a high achiever, someone who prided himself on his ability to control every aspect of his life. But when he lost his job unexpectedly, he found himself spiraling into despair, struggling to accept a reality he had never anticipated. For weeks, Marcus fought against his circumstances, replaying events in his mind, blaming himself, and fearing the future. But then he came across Epictetus' teachings on acceptance, on the idea that peace comes not from controlling every outcome but from releasing the need to do so.

Inspired by this philosophy, Marcus decided to let go of his desire to change the past. He shifted his focus to the present moment, asking himself what actions he could take to move forward rather than dwelling on what he had lost. Over time, this shift in perspective brought him a sense of peace, a calm he had never known before. He learned that acceptance is not about giving up; it's about embracing life's unpredictability with resilience and grace.

Epictetus' wisdom on acceptance is not only applicable in moments of loss but also in the daily stresses and frustrations we all face. By practicing acceptance, we free ourselves from the mental struggle that often accompanies unmet expectations or unanticipated changes. Instead of seeing acceptance as weakness, Epictetus invites us to view it as strength—a strength that allows us to navigate life's storms without being overwhelmed by them.

This approach gives us the ability to face each moment with an open heart and a steady mind, knowing that our peace does not depend on the world conforming to our desires but on our willingness to adapt to the world as it is.

Another enduring teaching of Epictetus is his insight into emotional resilience—the ability to face life's challenges with inner strength and composure. He taught that while emotions such as anger, fear, and sadness are natural, we do not have to be controlled by them.

Epictetus saw that many of our emotional reactions stem from our judgments, from the stories we tell ourselves about what events mean. By learning to question these judgments, to challenge our initial assumptions, we gain the ability to respond to life's challenges with calm and clarity rather than with impulsive reactions.

This approach to emotional resilience is invaluable in a world where stress, anxiety, and pressure are often unavoidable. Epictetus shows us that while we may not be able to eliminate these challenges, we can learn to face them with a sense of inner stability.

To build emotional resilience, Epictetus encouraged his students to cultivate a sense of detachment, a mental distance that allows us to observe our emotions without becoming entangled in them.

He taught that by learning to step back, to observe our feelings rather than identifying with them, we gain the freedom to choose our response. For example, when we feel anger rising, instead of reacting impulsively, we can pause, breathe, and ask ourselves if our reaction is serving us or if it is simply a habitual response. This pause allows us to respond with intention, choosing actions that reflect our values rather than being swept away by our emotions.

By practicing emotional detachment, we develop a resilience that enables us to face life's ups and downs with equanimity, a calm that is grounded in our own choices rather than in the external world.

Epictetus also believed that gratitude is essential for a fulfilling life. He taught that by focusing on what we have rather than on what we lack, we cultivate a mindset of abundance and contentment. In his view, gratitude is not just a pleasant feeling but a practice, a way of shifting our perspective from scarcity to appreciation.

By taking time each day to reflect on the things we are grateful for, we create a sense of inner wealth, a joy that is independent of material possessions or external success. This practice of gratitude is a reminder that happiness is not found in acquiring more but in appreciating what we already have.

In today's world, where consumerism often leads us to believe that happiness lies in more possessions, more achievements, more success, Epictetus' teaching on gratitude offers a powerful counterpoint. He reminds us that true wealth is not about what we own but about how we experience life.

By cultivating gratitude, we free ourselves from the constant desire for more, allowing us to find joy in each moment, in each small gift life offers. This shift in focus brings a profound peace, a sense of fulfillment that remains steady regardless of external circumstances.

To incorporate gratitude into your daily life, consider keeping a gratitude journal. Each day, take a few minutes to write down three things you are grateful for, whether they are big or small. Reflect on how these experiences contribute to your well-being, allowing yourself to feel a sense of appreciation for each one.

Over time, this practice of gratitude becomes a habit, a lens through which you view life with greater resilience and joy. By grounding yourself in gratitude, you create a mindset of abundance, a sense of inner wealth that enriches your life in every moment.

Epictetus also believed in the power of self-discipline, the ability to choose actions that align with our values even when they are difficult. He taught that self-discipline is the foundation of a life well-lived, a quality that allows us to pursue our goals with consistency and resilience.

In his view, self-discipline is not about rigid control but about making choices that reflect our true intentions, about choosing long-term fulfillment over short-term gratification. This approach to self-discipline is especially relevant in a world that often prioritizes instant rewards over lasting growth. Epictetus reminds us that the path to a meaningful life requires patience, commitment, and the courage to pursue our highest aspirations.

To build self-discipline, Epictetus encouraged his students to set clear intentions, to define what they wanted to achieve and to commit to their goals with integrity.

He believed that by setting intentions, we create a roadmap for our lives, a guide that helps us navigate the distractions and temptations that might otherwise pull us off course. In practical terms, this might mean setting a goal to improve a skill, to cultivate a healthy habit, or to deepen a relationship.

By committing to these goals, by taking small, consistent steps toward them each day, we build the self-discipline that enables us to live with purpose and resilience.

In the end, Epictetus' wisdom offers us a path to a life of peace, resilience, and fulfillment. Through his teachings, we learn that true freedom lies not in controlling the world but in mastering ourselves, that happiness is not found in external success but in inner contentment.

By practicing mindfulness, acceptance, emotional resilience, gratitude, and self-discipline, we create a life that is grounded in purpose, a life that reflects the timeless wisdom of Stoic philosophy. Through the practical application of Epictetus' teachings, we discover that we have the power to shape our own experience, to build a life of meaning and joy, and to face life's challenges with a heart that is steady and a mind that is clear.

Quotes

Epictetus & Marcus Aurelius

"A man's worth is no greater than the worth of his ambitions."

"A person's worth is measured by the worth of what he values."

"A wrongdoer is often a person who has left something undone, not always one who has done something."

"Accept the things to which fate binds you, and love the people with whom fate brings you together, but do so with all your heart."

"Adapt yourself to the things among which your lot has been cast and love sincerely the fellow creatures with whom destiny has ordained that you shall live."

"Be like the cliff against which the waves continually break; but it stands firm and tames the fury of the water around it."

"Begin each day by telling yourself: Today I shall be meeting with interference, ingratitude, insolence, disloyalty, ill-will, and selfishness—all of them due to the offender's ignorance of what is good or evil."

"Confine yourself to the present."

"Death smiles at us all, but all a man can do is smile back."

"Do every act of your life as though it were the very last act of your life."

"Do not act as if you were going to live ten thousand years. Death hangs over you. While you live, while it is in your power, be good."

"Do not be perturbed, for all things are according to the nature of the universal."

"Do not think that what is hard for you to master is humanly impossible; but if a thing is humanly possible, consider it to be within your reach."

"Dwell on the beauty of life. Watch the stars, and see yourself running with them."

"Every living organism is fulfilled when it follows the right path for its own nature."

"Everything we hear is an opinion, not a fact. Everything we see is a perspective, not the truth."

"He who fears death will never do anything worthy of a man who is alive."

"He who lives in harmony with himself lives in harmony with the universe."

"Here is a rule to remember in future, when anything tempts you to feel bitter: not, 'This is misfortune,' but 'To bear this worthily is good fortune.'"

"How absurd and ridiculous it is to be surprised at anything which happens in life!"

"How much more grievous are the consequences of anger than the causes of it."

"How much time he saves who does not look to see what his neighbor says or does or thinks."

"How ridiculous and how strange to be surprised at anything which happens in life."

"If it is not right, do not do it; if it is not true, do not say it."

"If you are pained by external things, it is not they that disturb you, but your own judgment of them. And it is in your power to wipe out that judgment now."

"If you do the job in a principled way, with diligence, energy, and patience, if you keep yourself free of distractions, and keep the spirit inside you undamaged, as if you might have to give it back at any moment—if you can embrace this without fear or expectation—can find fulfillment in what you're doing now, as Nature intended."

"It is not events that disturb people, it is their judgments concerning them."

"It is not the man who has too little, but the man who craves more, that is poor."

"Life is neither good nor evil, but only a place for good and evil."

"Look well into thyself; there is a source of strength which will always spring up if thou wilt always look."

"Loss is nothing else but change, and change is Nature's delight."

"Nothing happens to any man that he is not formed by nature to bear."

"Our life is what our thoughts make it."

"People are not disturbed by things, but by the views they take of them."

"Perfection of character is this: to live each day as if it were your last, without frenzy, without apathy, without pretense."

"Receive without conceit, release without struggle."

"Reject your sense of injury, and the injury itself disappears."

"Stop whatever you're doing for a moment and ask yourself: Am I afraid of death because I won't be able to do this anymore?"

"The art of living is more like wrestling than dancing."

"The best revenge is to be unlike him who performed the injury."

"The happiness of those who want to be popular depends on others; the happiness of those who seek pleasure fluctuates with moods outside their control; but the happiness of the wise grows out of their own free acts."

"The happiness of your life depends upon the quality of your thoughts."

"The impediment to action advances action. What stands in the way becomes the way."

"The object of life is not to be on the side of the majority but to escape finding oneself in the ranks of the insane."

"The only wealth which you will keep forever is the wealth you have given away."

"The soul becomes dyed with the color of its thoughts."

"The things you think about determine the quality of your mind."

"The tranquility that comes when you stop caring what they say. Or think, or do. Only what you do."

"The universe is transformation: life is opinion."

"Think of yourself as dead. You have lived your life. Now, take what's left and live it properly."

"To live a good life: We have the potential for it. If we learn to be indifferent to what makes no difference."

"To live happily is an inward power of the soul."

"To love only what happens, what was destined. No greater harmony."

"To refrain from imitation is the best revenge."

"To the wise, life is a problem; to the fool, a solution."

"To understand the true quality of people, you must look into their minds, and examine their pursuits and aversions."

"Very little is needed to make a happy life; it is all within yourself, in your way of thinking."

"Waste no more time arguing about what a good man should be. Be one."

"We are more often frightened than hurt; and we suffer more in imagination than in reality."

"We live only now. Everything else is either passed or is unknown."

"We ought to do good to others as simply as a horse runs, or a bee makes honey, or a vine bears grapes season after season without thinking of the grapes it has borne."

"What we do now echoes in eternity."

"When you arise in the morning, think of what a precious privilege it is to be alive—to breathe, to think, to enjoy, to love."

"When you wake up in the morning, tell yourself: The people I deal with today will be meddling, ungrateful, arrogant, dishonest, jealous, and surly."

"Whenever you are about to find fault with someone, ask yourself the following question: What fault of mine most nearly resembles the one I am about to criticize?"

"You always own the option of having no opinion."

"You could leave life right now. Let that determine what you do and say and think."

"You have power over your mind—not outside events. Realize this, and you will find strength."

"The best way to avenge yourself is not to be like that."

"Our life is what our thoughts make it."

"It is not death that a man should fear, but he should fear never beginning to live."

"Waste no more time arguing what a good man should be. Be one."

Bonus Chapter One

The Psychology of Stoicism— Applying Epictetus' Teachings to Modern Mental Health

In a world where mental health challenges like anxiety, stress, and overthinking are at an all-time high, ancient wisdom often finds a surprising home in modern practices. Epictetus, one of the most influential Stoic philosophers, taught principles that resonate deeply with today's psychological frameworks. His philosophy, rooted in the mastery of thoughts and emotions, laid the groundwork for many modern approaches to mental well-being. Among these is cognitive behavioral therapy (CBT), a widely used mental health intervention that directly parallels Stoic teachings.

Epictetus famously stated, "It is not what happens to you, but how you react to it that matters." This simple yet profound idea reflects the foundation of CBT, which emphasizes the power of our thoughts in shaping our emotional experiences. By learning to recognize and challenge unhelpful thought patterns, we can break free from cycles of anxiety and stress. This chapter explores how Epictetus' philosophy intersects with modern psychology and provides practical tools for readers to apply these timeless principles to their own mental health.

Introduction to Stoic Psychology

At its core, Stoic psychology revolves around the idea that our emotions and reactions are not dictated by external events but by our interpretations of those events. Epictetus taught that the mind has the power to control its response to any situation, no matter how challenging. This idea forms the backbone of CBT, a therapeutic approach that helps individuals identify and reframe distorted thinking patterns.

For example, a common cognitive distortion in modern psychology is catastrophizing—expecting the worst possible outcome in any situation. Epictetus addressed this tendency centuries ago, encouraging his students to examine their fears and challenge irrational beliefs. He asked them to consider: Is this fear grounded in reality? What is the worst that could happen, and how likely is it? This practice of questioning one's thoughts is central to both Stoicism and CBT, showing how closely aligned the two approaches are.

Modern psychology also emphasizes the importance of acceptance—a concept deeply embedded in Stoic philosophy. Epictetus taught that we must distinguish between what we can control and what we cannot, a principle known as the "dichotomy of control." This concept is echoed in mindfulness practices, which encourage individuals to let go of their attachment to uncontrollable outcomes and focus on what lies within their sphere of influence.

Practical Exercises Inspired by Epictetus and CBT

The practicality of Epictetus' teachings lies in their direct application to daily life. By integrating Stoic exercises with CBT techniques, readers can develop tools to manage their thoughts and emotions more effectively. Here are three exercises inspired by both Stoicism and modern psychology:

The Thought Journal: Challenging Negative Beliefs

Epictetus' Insight: "If you are pained by any external thing, it is not this thing that disturbs you, but your own judgment about it."

Exercise: Keep a journal to track your negative thoughts. Write down the situation, your initial reaction, and the emotions it triggered. Then, challenge these thoughts by asking: Is this belief based on facts? What alternative explanations could there be? What advice would I give a friend in this situation? By reframing your thoughts, you can shift your emotional response and reduce anxiety.

Premeditation of Evils: Preparing for Challenges

Epictetus' Insight: "When you are about to embark on any action, remind yourself what kind of action it is."

Exercise: Before facing a potentially stressful situation, visualize the possible challenges you might encounter and how you could respond. This technique, known as *premeditatio malorum* in Stoicism, allows you to prepare mentally for adversity, reducing its impact when it occurs. For instance, if you are nervous about a job interview, imagine scenarios where you face difficult questions and rehearse calm, confident responses.

The Serenity Reflection: Letting Go of the Uncontrollable

Epictetus' Insight: "Make the best use of what is in your power, and take the rest as it happens."

Exercise: At the end of each day, reflect on situations where you felt stressed or anxious. Ask yourself: Was this within my control? If not, what can I do to accept it and let it go? Use this exercise to practice the dichotomy of control, focusing your energy on what truly matters and releasing the rest.

Insights from Modern Psychologists

Many contemporary psychologists recognize the enduring relevance of Stoic philosophy in addressing mental health challenges. Dr. Donald Robertson, a cognitive behavioral therapist and author of *How to Think Like a Roman Emperor*, often highlights the direct connection between Stoicism and CBT. "The Stoics were the original cognitive therapists," he explains. "They understood that by changing our thoughts, we can change how we feel."

Another psychologist, Dr. Sharon Lebell, emphasizes the practical nature of Epictetus' teachings. "Epictetus offers us a manual for living," she says. "His philosophy is not about abstract ideas but about how to navigate the messiness of life with grace and resilience."

Modern practitioners frequently incorporate Stoic principles into their therapeutic approaches, particularly when working with clients struggling with anxiety and overthinking. For example, mindfulness-based cognitive therapy (MBCT) combines the Stoic practice of self-awareness with CBT techniques, encouraging individuals to observe their thoughts without judgment and challenge distorted beliefs.

One case study involves a client named Sarah, who suffered from chronic anxiety about her performance at work. Her therapist introduced her to the Stoic exercise of *premeditatio malorum*, encouraging her to visualize potential challenges and prepare for them mentally. Over time, Sarah learned to approach her work with greater confidence, accepting that while she could not control every outcome, she could control her effort and attitude. This shift in perspective reduced her anxiety and improved her overall well-being.

The Long-Term Benefits of Applying Epictetus' Teachings

The beauty of Epictetus' philosophy lies in its timeless relevance. While CBT provides short-term strategies for managing mental health, Stoicism offers a lifelong framework for building resilience and inner peace. By practicing Epictetus' teachings, individuals can develop the skills needed to navigate life's challenges with grace and clarity.

One of the key benefits of applying Stoic principles is the cultivation of emotional resilience. By focusing on what lies within their control, individuals can reduce the impact of external stressors and maintain a sense of stability even in uncertain times. This resilience is particularly valuable in today's fast-paced world, where individuals are constantly bombarded by external pressures and distractions.

Another benefit is the development of self-mastery. Epictetus taught that true freedom comes from mastering one's thoughts and actions, a concept that aligns closely with modern psychology's emphasis on self-regulation. By practicing self-discipline and mindfulness, individuals can gain greater control over their emotional responses, leading to a more balanced and fulfilling life.

Finally, Epictetus' teachings encourage individuals to embrace uncertainty and find peace in the present moment. This perspective is especially relevant in the context of mindfulness, which has become a cornerstone of modern mental health practices. By accepting life's unpredictability and focusing on what they can control, individuals can cultivate a sense of serenity that transcends external circumstances.

Conclusion: Bridging Ancient Wisdom and Modern Practice

Epictetus' philosophy offers a profound framework for understanding and improving mental health, one that remains deeply relevant in the modern world. His teachings on control, acceptance, and resilience provide practical tools for managing anxiety, overthinking, and stress, while his emphasis on self-mastery and mindfulness resonates with contemporary psychological practices.

By bridging the wisdom of Epictetus with the principles of CBT, this chapter highlights the enduring power of Stoicism as a guide to mental well-being. Whether you are navigating personal challenges, seeking greater clarity, or striving for emotional resilience, Epictetus' teachings offer a roadmap to a more balanced and fulfilling life. His message is simple yet profound: while we cannot control the world around us, we can control how we respond—and in that response lies our freedom.

Bonus Chapter Two

The Art of Letting Go— Epictetus' Teachings on Control, Acceptance, and Serenity

Focus: A focused exploration of Epictetus' insights on letting go of things beyond one's control, a theme with universal appeal.

Outline:

Understanding Control vs. Acceptance: A breakdown of Epictetus' teachings on the dichotomy of control, with relatable modern examples.

Practical "Letting Go" Exercises: Guided practices inspired by Epictetus to help readers apply this philosophy in moments of stress, loss, or change.

Long-Term Benefits of Acceptance: Insights into how accepting life's unpredictability can lead to lasting serenity and resilience.

Value: This chapter is practical and actionable, ideal for readers looking to integrate Stoic wisdom into daily life as a path to greater peace and emotional resilience.

One of Epictetus' most profound insights is deceptively simple: to cultivate a peaceful life, focus only on what lies within your control, and let go of what does not. This principle is the cornerstone of Stoic philosophy, providing a pathway to serenity and resilience amidst life's inevitable uncertainties. Epictetus believed that many of our anxieties stem from trying to control the uncontrollable—from worrying about others' opinions to resisting inevitable changes. Through acceptance and a disciplined focus on self-mastery, he taught that true freedom lies not in changing our circumstances, but in changing our response to them.

In a world that values productivity and control, the art of letting go can seem counterintuitive. We are often taught to assert influence, to strive, to achieve. Yet, paradoxically, it is in releasing our grip on external circumstances and shifting our attention inward that we find the peace we seek. This chapter explores Epictetus' teachings on control, acceptance, and serenity, offering practical insights and exercises to help readers integrate these ideas into daily life, fostering a mindset of calm, resilience, and inner strength.

Understanding Control vs. Acceptance

At the heart of Epictetus' philosophy is the *dichotomy of control*, the distinction between what is within our power and what is beyond it. He emphasized that our minds and actions—our thoughts, judgments, decisions, and responses—are entirely within our control. Everything else, including external events, the actions of others, and the outcome of our efforts, remains beyond our influence. By accepting this reality, we can free ourselves from needless frustration and anxiety, redirecting our energy toward what truly matters.

Epictetus illustrated this idea with a simple metaphor: life is like a banquet. When dishes are passed to you, take a portion with gratitude. If a dish bypasses you, let it pass without disappointment. This metaphor reflects the balance of action and acceptance, reminding us that while we may reach for what we desire, we must also gracefully accept what we cannot have. It is a practice of embracing life's offerings without clinging, knowing that contentment comes not from grasping but from a mindful and balanced approach to life.

Consider how this principle applies in today's world, where we often try to control outcomes, manage perceptions, and secure our future. For instance, we might worry about how others perceive us, striving to project a perfect image. Yet Epictetus would argue that others' opinions are outside our control, and that real freedom lies in focusing on our own integrity and actions. When we let go of the need to control others' perceptions, we experience a profound sense of release, grounded in the assurance that we are enough as we are. Acceptance of this fact frees us from a life spent in pursuit of validation, allowing us to engage more fully and authentically with the present moment.

Similarly, in relationships, we often attempt to influence the behavior and attitudes of those we love. Epictetus teaches us that while we can encourage, support, and advise, we cannot change others. By recognizing the limits of our influence, we can practice compassion without expectation, fostering relationships built on respect rather than control. This approach liberates us from the emotional burden of disappointment, helping us to cultivate deeper, more harmonious connections with others.

Practical "Letting Go" Exercises

To apply Epictetus' teachings, the following exercises can serve as practical tools for letting go of control, embracing acceptance, and finding peace. These practices are designed to foster a Stoic mindset, helping readers approach life's challenges with resilience and calm.

The Circle of Control Exercise Start by drawing two concentric circles on a piece of paper. In the inner circle, list everything within your control—your thoughts, actions, responses, and attitudes. In the outer circle, write down what lies beyond your control, such as others' opinions, past events, and natural outcomes. Take a moment to reflect on how much energy you've spent worrying about things in the outer circle. Commit to focusing only on what's inside the inner circle, reminding yourself that your peace lies in mastering what is within your power. This exercise can be revisited regularly, especially during times of stress. By visualizing what you can control, you strengthen your ability to let go of concerns over the uncontrollable, gradually developing a mindset of acceptance and resilience.

Reframing Setbacks Epictetus often emphasized that it's not events themselves that disturb us, but our judgments about them. In this exercise, choose a recent setback or challenge that caused frustration. Reflect on how you initially perceived the event—did you see it as a failure, a setback, or an obstacle? Now, try to reframe the event by considering it from a new perspective: What lesson might it offer? How can it strengthen you? By reframing setbacks, you develop a habit of viewing challenges not as hindrances but as opportunities for growth, an essential skill in cultivating Stoic resilience. This exercise helps you build the practice of releasing your attachment to specific outcomes. Instead of seeing a situation as "good" or "bad," you begin to view life's events as part of a larger tapestry, each experience adding depth to your character and understanding.

Mindful "Letting Go" Meditation Sit in a quiet place, close your eyes, and take several deep breaths. With each exhale, consciously release a worry or concern that you cannot control. Visualize these worries as leaves floating down a stream, gradually moving out of sight. As each worry leaves, affirm, "I release what I cannot control; I focus on what I can." This meditation helps train your mind to recognize and release the mental clutter of uncontrollable concerns, allowing you to focus more fully on the present moment and your own agency within it. Practicing this meditation daily, even for a few minutes, can bring a profound sense of calm. It helps reinforce the habit of letting go, reminding you that peace is a choice that comes from within.

Long-Term Benefits of Acceptance

The long-term benefits of practicing control and acceptance extend beyond personal serenity; they contribute to emotional resilience, mental clarity, and a deeper connection with life's purpose. When we accept life's uncertainties, we free ourselves from the mental exhaustion of constant resistance, allowing us to navigate challenges with a steady mind and an open heart.

Resilience Through Change Life is constantly evolving, and the ability to adapt is essential for resilience. Epictetus taught that resistance to change creates suffering, while acceptance fosters peace. By letting go of the need for life to unfold according to our desires, we cultivate a flexibility that allows us to adapt gracefully to new circumstances. This resilience is not passive resignation; it is an active choice to embrace life's flux with courage and faith, trusting in our own ability to navigate whatever comes our way. For example, consider the common experience of career transitions. A sudden job loss or unexpected career shift can trigger fear and insecurity, as we grapple with the loss of control. By applying Epictetus' teachings, we can reframe these events as opportunities for growth, focusing on what lies within our control—our response, adaptability, and openness to new possibilities. This shift in perspective transforms fear into opportunity, empowering us to approach change with confidence.

Freedom from Anxiety Many of our anxieties stem from an excessive focus on outcomes beyond our control. Epictetus observed that when we release our attachment to specific results, we open ourselves to a state of inner freedom. Acceptance helps us recognize that our peace does not depend on circumstances but on our ability to live in harmony with reality. This shift in mindset allows us to approach life with a calm spirit, reducing the stress and anxiety that arise from the need to control every detail. In our daily lives, this principle can be applied to everything from project deadlines to family dynamics. Instead of worrying about whether everything will go as planned, we can focus on doing our best with the resources and knowledge we have. Letting go of the need for perfection frees us from the grip of anxiety, creating space for joy, spontaneity, and deeper engagement with the present.

Deepening Relationships Through Acceptance One of the most transformative benefits of acceptance is its impact on relationships. By letting go of the need to control others' actions or beliefs, we cultivate a mindset of respect and empathy. This openness fosters authentic connections, as we allow others the freedom to be themselves without judgment or expectation. Epictetus taught that we cannot dictate the actions of others, but we can choose how we engage with them, creating relationships built on understanding rather than control. In practice, this means embracing others' individuality and letting go of the urge to "fix" or change them. It allows us to experience deeper, more harmonious relationships, grounded in mutual respect and acceptance. By focusing on our own behavior, we become positive influences in the lives of others, encouraging their growth without imposing our own desires or judgments.

A Life of Serenity Through Letting Go

Epictetus' teachings on control and acceptance are more than philosophical ideals; they are practical tools for creating a life of serenity, resilience, and purpose. The art of letting go is not about giving up; it is about living fully in the present, free from the weight of expectations and attachments. This mindset enables us to approach life's ups and downs with an open heart, knowing that our inner peace is rooted in our response, not in our circumstances.

By embracing Epictetus' wisdom, we come to understand that true freedom lies not in changing the world around us, but in changing our relationship to it. Acceptance becomes a source of strength, allowing us to move through life with grace and confidence, no matter what challenges we encounter. In a world that often feels chaotic and unpredictable, Epictetus offers a path to a deeper peace, showing us that by letting go of what we cannot control, we gain everything that truly matters.

Through the practice of letting go, we are invited to step into the present moment, fully alive, fully engaged, and fully free.

Bonus Chapter Three

Epictetus and Leadership— How the Stoic Path Shapes Resilient Leaders

The teachings of Epictetus have endured not only because of their wisdom but because of their profound applicability to the art of leadership. From the time of his exile in Nicopolis, where he attracted young minds and emerging leaders, to the present day, Epictetus' insights on self-mastery, integrity, and resilience have inspired individuals tasked with leading others. His influence is seen in the reflections of Emperor Marcus Aurelius, in the writings of Enlightenment philosophers, and in the practices of modern CEOs and political figures who navigate complex, high-stakes decisions. In this chapter, we'll explore how Epictetus' teachings have shaped leaders throughout history and how his principles can provide a powerful framework for those seeking to lead with resilience and integrity in the modern world.

Leadership is often seen as a role of control and power, but for Epictetus, true leadership is about inner mastery. He believed that the strength of a leader lies not in their ability to command others, but in their ability to command themselves. His teachings offer a roadmap for cultivating the kind of character that inspires loyalty, trust, and respect—qualities that remain timeless in their appeal and relevance. In an age when leadership is often associated with external success, Epictetus reminds us that true greatness lies within, in the ability to face adversity with courage, make difficult decisions with integrity, and lead others with humility and purpose.

Historical Leaders Inspired by Epictetus

Epictetus' first and perhaps most famous disciple was Marcus Aurelius, who would go on to become one of Rome's most revered emperors and one of history's most respected philosopher-kings. Marcus discovered Epictetus' teachings during a time of personal and political challenges. He ruled an empire constantly threatened by internal division and external threats, and he knew that the stability of Rome depended on his ability to lead with wisdom and restraint. In his personal writings, *Meditations*, Marcus reflects on the Stoic principles of Epictetus, reminding himself to remain calm amidst chaos, to seek virtue over praise, and to approach each decision with clarity and purpose. "Waste no more time arguing what a good man should be. Be one," he wrote—a line that embodies Epictetus' emphasis on living one's principles rather than merely espousing them.

Marcus Aurelius' legacy as a Stoic leader is defined by his commitment to duty and humility, qualities he drew from Epictetus' teachings. He understood that leadership was not about personal power or prestige, but about serving the greater good and maintaining inner stability even in the face of adversity. This approach to leadership has resonated through the ages, inspiring countless leaders who seek to embody Stoic ideals of resilience, ethical decision-making, and dedication to their role.

The Enlightenment period brought a resurgence of interest in Stoic principles, particularly those of Epictetus. Thinkers like Thomas Jefferson, who drafted the American Declaration of Independence, were deeply influenced by Stoic ideas on freedom, responsibility, and self-governance. Jefferson, who admired Epictetus and other Stoic philosophers, saw in their teachings a foundation for the ethical and intellectual autonomy that would become central to American identity. Stoic values of personal accountability and self-mastery became ideals for the new nation, reflecting Epictetus' belief that true freedom is not granted by others but cultivated within.

In the 20th century, President Ronald Reagan provided a modern example of Stoic leadership in his approach to U.S.-Soviet relations, particularly during his negotiations with Soviet Premier Mikhail Gorbachev. Reagan, known for his strength of character and unwavering commitment to freedom, approached these high-stakes discussions with a blend of firm principles and strategic flexibility—qualities Epictetus would have recognized as essential for a true leader. At a time when the world was shadowed by nuclear tension, Reagan demonstrated a level of patience, clarity, and resilience that helped usher in an era of reduced hostilities.

Reagan's famous line, "Trust, but verify," echoed Epictetus' belief in grounded trust, marked by caution and awareness. This phrase became a cornerstone of his negotiations with Gorbachev, embodying a Stoic balance between openness and vigilance. Reagan's Stoic-like wisdom was evident in his ability to maintain a clear focus on long-term peace and security, without allowing his decisions to be influenced by emotions or political pressure. He once said, "There is no limit to what a man can do or where he can go if he doesn't mind who gets the credit." This humility and focus on purpose over personal glory reflect a Stoic approach to leadership, emphasizing the role of service over self-promotion.

During his exchanges with Gorbachev, Reagan held firmly to his values of freedom and democracy, refusing to compromise on these core beliefs. Yet he remained open to dialogue, demonstrating the Stoic principle of resilience—standing firm in his principles while engaging with his perceived adversary in constructive conversation. By focusing on what he could control—his own diplomatic approach and commitment to values—Reagan contributed to significant arms reduction agreements, such as the Intermediate-Range Nuclear Forces (INF) Treaty, which marked a critical step in ending the Cold War. His resilience and calm in navigating these tense discussions showed how Stoic principles could be applied to create lasting positive change, even under the most pressurized conditions.

The Enlightenment period brought a resurgence of interest in Stoic principles, particularly those of Epictetus. Thinkers like Thomas Jefferson, who drafted the American Declaration of Independence, were deeply influenced by Stoic ideas on freedom, responsibility, and self-governance. Jefferson, who admired Epictetus and other Stoic philosophers, saw in their teachings a foundation for the ethical and intellectual autonomy that would become central to American identity. Stoic values of personal accountability and self-mastery became ideals for the new nation, reflecting Epictetus' belief that true freedom is not granted by others but cultivated within.

In the business world, leaders like Warren Buffett have championed principles that align closely with Epictetus' Stoic philosophy. Buffett's emphasis on long-term thinking, ethical decision-making, and emotional discipline has set him apart in an industry often defined by quick wins and high volatility. By focusing on what he can control—his actions, choices, and ethical standards—Buffett exemplifies the Stoic principle of self-mastery. Like Epictetus, he views external circumstances as secondary to the values and virtues that guide his actions. Buffett's approach is a modern-day application of Epictetus' teaching: "Make the best use of what is in your power, and take the rest as it happens."

In the business world, leaders like Warren Buffett have championed principles that align closely with Epictetus' Stoic philosophy. Buffett's emphasis on long-term thinking, ethical decision-making, and emotional discipline has set him apart in an industry often defined by quick wins and high volatility. By focusing on what he can control—his actions, choices, and ethical standards—Buffett exemplifies the Stoic principle of self-mastery. Like Epictetus, he views external circumstances as secondary to the values and virtues that guide his actions. Buffett's approach is a modern-day application of Epictetus' teaching: "Make the best use of what is in your power, and take the rest as it happens."

Leadership Lessons from Epictetus

Epictetus' philosophy provides a set of core lessons that can serve as guiding principles for effective leadership. These lessons are not theoretical ideals, but practical tools that leaders can use to cultivate inner resilience, make ethical decisions, and inspire those they lead. By embodying these principles, leaders can navigate the complexities of their roles with clarity and purpose.

Resilience in Adversity: Epictetus taught that adversity is an inevitable part of life and that our response to it defines our character. He urged his followers to view challenges as opportunities to practice resilience, to test and refine their virtues. For leaders, this means facing crises not as insurmountable obstacles but as chances to demonstrate calm, patience, and resourcefulness. By embracing adversity as a natural part of their journey, leaders can cultivate the inner strength needed to remain steady and effective under pressure.

Focus on What You Can Control: One of Epictetus' most profound teachings is the dichotomy of control—the distinction between what lies within our control and what does not. He taught that by focusing on our own thoughts, actions, and decisions, we free ourselves from the anxiety of trying to control external events. For leaders, this principle is invaluable. In a world where many factors are outside their control, focusing on what they can influence—their behavior, their ethics, their decisions—allows leaders to act with clarity and purpose, unburdened by the need to control every outcome.

Ethical Integrity: Epictetus believed that virtue was the foundation of a meaningful life, and this principle is equally vital for leadership. Ethical integrity means making decisions that align with one's values, even when they may be unpopular or difficult. Leaders who prioritize ethics over expediency inspire trust and loyalty, as their actions are rooted in principles rather than self-interest. For Epictetus, true leadership is not about pursuing power but about embodying values that benefit the greater good.

Emotional Discipline: Epictetus understood that emotions are natural, but he believed that leaders must learn to govern their reactions. Emotional discipline allows leaders to make decisions from a place of clarity rather than reacting impulsively to situations. This does not mean suppressing emotions, but rather cultivating an awareness that allows one to respond thoughtfully. Leaders who practice emotional discipline inspire confidence, as they can be trusted to remain calm and measured, even in the face of difficult situations.

Humility and Self-Awareness: For Epictetus, humility was not a sign of weakness but of wisdom. He taught that true knowledge comes from understanding one's limitations and constantly seeking improvement. Leaders who embrace humility are open to learning and growth, viewing their role not as a position of superiority but as a responsibility to serve and uplift others. This humility fosters self-awareness, a quality that allows leaders to recognize their strengths and weaknesses and to lead with authenticity and empathy.

Stoic Leadership Exercises

To put Epictetus' teachings into practice, here are some exercises that leaders can use to cultivate the Stoic qualities of resilience, integrity, and focus:

Daily Reflection: Each evening, take a few minutes to reflect on the day's events, focusing on how you responded to challenges. Ask yourself: Did I act with integrity? Did I remain calm under pressure? How did I handle what was within my control? This practice of self-reflection helps reinforce the values you aim to embody, encouraging you to approach each day with a mindset of growth and accountability.

Pre-meditation of Adversity: Known as *premeditatio malorum*, this exercise involves imagining potential challenges you may face and rehearsing how you would respond. For example, before a critical meeting, consider the possible objections or setbacks that could arise and mentally prepare to respond with calm and integrity. This practice fosters resilience by reducing the element of surprise and enabling you to face difficulties with a composed and prepared mind.

Emotional Check-ins: Throughout the day, take brief moments to check in with your emotions. Ask yourself: Am I reacting or responding? Am I letting external events dictate my mood? By cultivating this awareness, you can learn to pause before reacting, allowing you to make decisions from a place of calm and clarity rather than from impulsive emotion.

Weekly Review of Values: Dedicate time each week to revisit your core values and assess how well your recent actions have aligned with them. Reflect on any moments where you may have compromised your principles and consider how you might approach similar situations differently in the future. This exercise strengthens your commitment to ethical integrity, helping you stay grounded in your values regardless of external pressures.

The Circle of Control: Create a visual representation of what lies within your control and what does not. Draw a circle on a piece of paper and list everything you can control within the circle—your actions, your responses, your choices. Outside the circle, list factors beyond your control, such as others' opinions, external events, or outcomes. By focusing on what lies within the circle, you remind yourself to channel your energy where it has the most impact, reducing stress and increasing your sense of purpose.

The Enduring Value of Stoic Leadership

The teachings of Epictetus offer a powerful blueprint for modern leadership. At a time when many leaders are judged by their external achievements, Epictetus reminds us that true greatness lies in the strength of character. His philosophy teaches that leaders can be steady amidst the storm, ethical in the face of temptation, and resilient through hardship. By embodying these principles, leaders not only become more effective but also inspire those they lead to pursue lives of purpose, integrity, and resilience.

Today, Epictetus' teachings are more relevant than ever, offering timeless guidance for leaders who wish to make a meaningful impact. In a world of uncertainty, his philosophy is a source of clarity and strength, a reminder that true power is not found in control over others, but in mastery over oneself. As leaders continue to face the complexities of an ever-changing world, Epictetus' wisdom remains a beacon, illuminating the path to resilience, authenticity, and greatness.

By adopting the Stoic principles of Epictetus, leaders can transform themselves from managers of people to true stewards of virtue, integrity, and strength. This is the essence of Stoic leadership—a commitment not to power or authority, but to the pursuit of excellence in character, to the service of others, and to the unwavering belief that true freedom and leadership begin within.

In the 20th century, President Ronald Reagan provided a modern example of Stoic leadership in his approach to U.S.-Soviet relations, particularly during his negotiations with Soviet Premier Mikhail Gorbachev. Reagan, known for his strength of character and unwavering commitment to freedom, approached these high-stakes discussions with a blend of firm principles and strategic flexibility—qualities Epictetus would have recognized as essential for a true leader. At a time when the world was shadowed by nuclear tension, Reagan demonstrated a level of patience, clarity, and resilience that helped usher in an era of reduced hostilities.

Reagan's famous line, "Trust, but verify," echoed Epictetus' belief in grounded trust, marked by caution and awareness. This phrase became a cornerstone of his negotiations with Gorbachev, embodying a Stoic balance between openness and vigilance. Reagan's Stoic-like wisdom was evident in his ability to maintain a clear focus on long-term peace and security, without allowing his decisions to be influenced by emotions or political pressure. He once said, "There is no limit to what a man can do or where he can go if he doesn't mind who gets the credit." This humility and focus on purpose over personal glory reflect a Stoic approach to leadership, emphasizing the role of service over self-promotion.

During his exchanges with Gorbachev, Reagan held firmly to his values of freedom and democracy, refusing to compromise on these core beliefs. Yet he remained open to dialogue, demonstrating the Stoic principle of resilience—standing firm in his principles while engaging with his perceived adversary in constructive conversation. By focusing on what he could control—his own diplomatic approach and commitment to values—Reagan contributed to significant arms reduction agreements, such as the Intermediate-Range Nuclear Forces (INF) Treaty, which marked a critical step in ending the Cold War. His resilience and calm in navigating these tense discussions showed how Stoic principles could be applied to create lasting positive change, even under the most pressurized conditions.

The Enlightenment period brought a resurgence of interest in Stoic principles, particularly those of Epictetus. Thinkers like Thomas Jefferson, who drafted the American Declaration of Independence, were deeply influenced by Stoic ideas on freedom, responsibility, and self-governance. Jefferson, who admired Epictetus and other Stoic philosophers, saw in their teachings a foundation for the ethical and intellectual autonomy that would become central to American identity. Stoic values of personal accountability and self-mastery became ideals for the new nation, reflecting Epictetus' belief that true freedom is not granted by others but cultivated within.

In the business world, leaders like Warren Buffett have championed principles that align closely with Epictetus' Stoic philosophy. Buffett's emphasis on long-term thinking, ethical decision-making, and emotional discipline has set him apart in an industry often defined by quick wins and high volatility. By focusing on what he can control—his actions, choices, and ethical standards—Buffett exemplifies the Stoic principle of self-mastery. Like Epictetus, he views external circumstances as secondary to the values and virtues that guide his actions. Buffett's approach is a modern-day application of Epictetus' teaching: "Make the best use of what is in your power, and take the rest as it happens."

Bonus Chapter Four

Epictetus' Teachings in Action—Real-Life Stories of Modern-Day "Kings" Freed by Stoicism

Epictetus' teachings on resilience, acceptance, and inner freedom have resonated with readers for centuries. These principles are more than philosophical ideals; they are practical tools for overcoming adversity and finding peace amidst life's challenges. From high-stakes business leaders to athletes, artists, and everyday individuals, people across various walks of life have used Epictetus' teachings to reclaim their mental freedom, overcome setbacks, and cultivate resilience. This chapter shares a selection of stories from modern-day "kings"—individuals who have embraced Stoicism, not for fame or power, but to master themselves. Each story highlights a core Stoic principle in action, offering readers a living testament to the transformative power of Epictetus' philosophy.

Profiles of Modern Stoics

James Caldwell: The CEO Who Let Go of Control Principle: Focus on What You Can Control James Caldwell, a tech CEO, found himself at the helm of a rapidly growing company in Silicon Valley. As his company expanded, so did his stress. Caldwell constantly worried about external factors—investor opinions, competitors, and even the stock market's daily fluctuations. The pressure was relentless, and he began to lose sight of the reasons he started his company in the first place. After a particularly turbulent board meeting, Caldwell came across Epictetus' teaching, "Make the best use of what is in your power, and take the rest as it happens." Inspired, Caldwell began implementing Stoic practices, focusing on his responses and letting go of outcomes beyond his control. He started each day by writing down what he could influence—his actions, decisions, and the culture he fostered within his company. Over time, he stopped obsessing over external pressures and redirected his energy toward leading with integrity and purpose. This shift transformed not only Caldwell's outlook but also his company. By focusing on what he could control, he created a culture of resilience and trust, inspiring his team to thrive even during market fluctuations. Reflection: "Letting go of the need to control everything was freeing," Caldwell reflects. "I learned that I don't need to manage every outcome; I just need to stay true to my principles. Epictetus taught me that peace comes from within, not from circumstances."

Anna Morales: An Olympic Athlete's Path to Resilience Principle: Embrace Adversity as a Teacher Anna Morales, an Olympic swimmer, had trained her entire life for one goal: to win a gold medal. However, in the final round of the qualifiers, she suffered a shoulder injury that dashed her hopes of competing. For months, she struggled with disappointment, unable to come to terms with the loss. One day, her coach introduced her to the works of Epictetus, encouraging her to read his reflections on adversity. "Difficulties are things that show a person what they are," Epictetus wrote, a line that resonated deeply with Anna. She began to see her injury not as a setback but as an opportunity to grow. Instead of wallowing in frustration, she shifted her focus to recovery, training her mind as diligently as she once trained her body. She approached each day as a chance to cultivate inner resilience, embracing meditation and visualization techniques to strengthen her mindset. By the time she returned to the pool, Anna was not only physically prepared but mentally unbreakable, knowing that her strength came from within. Reflection: "Epictetus taught me to redefine adversity," says Morales. "I may never have won a gold medal, but I found something more valuable: resilience. That's a gift no one can take from me."

Sophie Kim: Finding Inner Peace in a Competitive World Principle: Detach from the Need for Validation Sophie Kim, a renowned classical pianist, faced a unique challenge. Known for her perfectionism, she frequently felt inadequate despite her success. Criticism, whether from music critics or social media comments, would haunt her, leaving her questioning her worth. Her constant need for external validation was affecting her mental health, and she began to lose her love for music. A friend recommended she read Epictetus, and one line struck her: "If you are ever tempted to look for outside approval, realize that you have compromised your integrity if you need praise from others." Sophie decided to take a different approach, focusing on playing music for the joy of it, rather than for others' approval. She set a simple intention before each performance: to express her art sincerely, without needing praise or fearing criticism. This shift allowed her to rediscover her passion for music, and as she detached from the need for validation, her performances became more authentic and moving. Epictetus' teachings freed her from the chains of external approval, allowing her to connect with her art and her audience on a deeper level. Reflection: "Epictetus helped me see that true freedom isn't found in applause," Kim shares. "It's found in creating from a place of honesty and letting go of what others think. My music has become a form of meditation."

David Chen: Overcoming Failure in Entrepreneurship Principle: Accept Setbacks and Move Forward David Chen, a young entrepreneur, launched a startup with high hopes, pouring all his resources and energy into its success. However, after a few years, his business failed, leaving him devastated and in debt. He felt like a failure and questioned his purpose. While seeking guidance, he stumbled upon Epictetus' teaching: "Remember, it is not events themselves that disturb us, but our interpretations of those events." David began to reframe his perspective on failure. Instead of viewing it as a reflection of his worth, he saw it as a learning experience, an opportunity to improve and grow. He spent time analyzing his mistakes, learning from them, and applying those lessons to new ventures. Embracing Epictetus' perspective on setbacks allowed David to let go of shame and move forward with renewed purpose. Today, he leads a successful company, attributing his resilience to Stoic philosophy and the lessons he learned from failure. Reflection: "Failing was painful, but it became a turning point. Epictetus taught me that failure isn't an end—it's a step in the process. I learned to detach my worth from my successes and setbacks."

Linda Rosario: A Mother's Journey Through Grief Principle: Find Peace in Acceptance Linda Rosario, a mother of three, faced a profound loss when her youngest child passed away due to illness. Overcome with grief, Linda struggled to find peace, feeling trapped in the pain of her loss. She attended grief counseling, where she was introduced to Epictetus' reflections on acceptance. His words, "Some things are up to us, and some things are not," resonated with her deeply. Linda began to work on accepting the reality of her loss, focusing on what was within her control—her memories, her love, and the support she could provide to her other children. She started a foundation in her daughter's memory, helping families navigate grief and loss. This act of acceptance transformed her suffering into purpose, allowing her to honor her daughter's legacy while finding a measure of peace. Reflection: "Epictetus showed me that acceptance is not about forgetting or moving on," Linda explains. "It's about embracing life as it is and finding ways to love, honor, and remember. That acceptance gave me strength."

Key Stoic Principles in Action

Each of these stories highlights a different Stoic principle, showing how Epictetus' teachings can be applied in real-life situations:

Focus on What You Can Control: James Caldwell's story of focusing only on his actions as a CEO shows how redirecting our energy toward what we can influence can reduce stress and increase effectiveness.

Embrace Adversity as a Teacher: Anna Morales' journey through injury demonstrates how adversity, rather than hindering us, can serve as a powerful catalyst for growth and resilience.

Detach from the Need for Validation: Sophie Kim's experience as a pianist reveals the freedom that comes from focusing on personal integrity rather than external approval.

Accept Setbacks and Move Forward: David Chen's resilience after failure illustrates the power of reframing setbacks as valuable lessons.

Find Peace in Acceptance: Linda Rosario's story of accepting loss underscores the healing potential of embracing life's inevitable challenges and finding purpose amidst grief.

Reflections and Lessons

These individuals' journeys reflect the timeless relevance of Epictetus' teachings. Each one faced unique challenges, yet all found freedom by applying Stoic principles in their own ways. Epictetus' wisdom on letting go of external concerns, embracing setbacks, and accepting life's natural course empowered them to reclaim peace and strength.

For readers, these stories offer a reminder that Stoicism is not a distant or abstract philosophy; it is a practical guide to living well, regardless of our circumstances. Whether we face professional challenges, personal losses, or internal struggles, Epictetus teaches us that freedom, resilience, and peace are within our reach. His insights remind us that we are not defined by what happens to us, but by how we choose to respond. And in this choice lies our true strength.

This chapter personalizes Epictetus' philosophy through relatable and inspiring stories, giving readers practical examples of Stoicism's transformative power.

Bonus Chapter Five

Epictetus' Philosophy on Freedom—Exploring the Boundaries of Mental Liberation

Epictetus, a man born into slavery, understood the paradox of freedom more profoundly than most. Despite living his early years as a slave, Epictetus believed and taught that true freedom does not come from external conditions but from within. According to him, real liberty is a product of the mind, and those who master their responses, emotions, and desires achieve a kind of freedom that no external force can take away. This philosophy of inner liberation became the bedrock of his teachings, inspiring individuals throughout history to embrace a resilient, unconquerable spirit. In this chapter, we will explore the boundaries of Epictetus' philosophy on freedom, examining how his ideas about mental liberation have transcended physical limitations, influenced movements for social justice, and offered hope and strength to those facing adversity.

Epictetus' concept of freedom was revolutionary for his time. In a world where freedom was largely defined by social status and political autonomy, Epictetus argued that mental freedom is the ultimate form of liberation. By distinguishing between what lies within our control (our thoughts, emotions, and actions) and what does not (external events and the actions of others), Epictetus reframed freedom as an internal achievement rather than an external condition. His teachings on freedom continue to resonate today, offering guidance for individuals navigating personal struggles, as well as communities striving for social and political justice.

Mental vs. Physical Freedom

Epictetus' teachings make a clear distinction between mental and physical freedom. Physical freedom, in the Stoic sense, pertains to our external circumstances—where we live, who governs us, and the social or political freedoms we enjoy or lack. Mental freedom, on the other hand, is entirely within our control. It is the capacity to choose our thoughts, shape our beliefs, and govern our emotional responses. For Epictetus, this internal freedom was far more valuable than any external liberty, as it could not be taken away by force or circumstance.

This concept of mental liberation has significant implications for modern struggles, particularly those concerning social justice, human rights, and personal autonomy. By emphasizing mental freedom, Epictetus does not dismiss the importance of physical freedom; rather, he offers a pathway to resilience for individuals and communities who face external oppression. He teaches us that while we may not always control the circumstances of our lives, we can control how we respond to them. This mindset has inspired countless individuals and movements to pursue both inner and outer liberation, with

Epictetus' teachings serving as a guiding force for those seeking justice and equality.

In the context of social justice, Epictetus' philosophy empowers individuals to reclaim agency over their own minds, regardless of external constraints. For those living in oppressive societies, facing systemic discrimination, or advocating for human rights, the Stoic concept of mental freedom provides a powerful foundation for resilience and perseverance. It encourages individuals to focus on what they can control—their values, actions, and sense of purpose—while working toward a vision of a just society. This mindset has supported and sustained activists, political prisoners, and marginalized communities in their pursuit of freedom, allowing them to cultivate inner strength in the face of adversity.

Case Studies of Mental Liberation

Throughout history, individuals have drawn on Epictetus' teachings to transcend physical limitations and achieve a sense of mental freedom. These stories of resilience demonstrate the transformative power of Stoic philosophy, illustrating how individuals from diverse backgrounds have used Epictetus' insights to reclaim their freedom, even under the most challenging circumstances.

1. James Stockdale: A Prisoner of War's Stoic Resilience

One of the most well-known examples of Stoic resilience inspired by Epictetus is the story of Admiral James Stockdale, a U.S. Navy officer who was held as a prisoner of war in Vietnam for over seven years. During his captivity, Stockdale endured unimaginable suffering, including torture and isolation. Yet, he found strength in Epictetus' teachings, which he had studied prior to his capture. Stockdale embraced the Stoic concept of focusing on what he could control—his own mind and attitude—while letting go of what was beyond his control.

Epictetus' teachings became a lifeline for Stockdale, who later credited Stoic philosophy with helping him survive the ordeal. He recounted how, despite the physical confinement, he experienced a profound sense of freedom by focusing on his inner strength and principles. Stockdale's resilience became known as the "Stockdale Paradox"—the ability to confront brutal reality while maintaining faith in one's capacity to endure. His story demonstrates how Epictetus' teachings can liberate the mind, even in the most oppressive conditions, offering a profound example of mental freedom in action.

2. Nelson Mandela: Freedom Beyond Bars

Nelson Mandela, who spent 27 years in prison for his role in the anti-apartheid movement in South Africa, embodied Epictetus' philosophy of mental liberation. Despite his physical confinement, Mandela cultivated a sense of inner freedom that allowed him to endure the hardships of prison life and emerge as a symbol of resilience and peace. He refused to let his captors break his spirit, instead using his time in prison to reflect, strengthen his resolve, and cultivate compassion.

Mandela's mental liberation was rooted in his ability to control his thoughts, emotions, and actions. He chose to see his imprisonment not as a defeat but as a time for growth, preparing himself to lead his country toward freedom and reconciliation. By embracing the Stoic principle of focusing on what he could control, Mandela transformed his suffering into a source of strength, demonstrating the power of mental freedom to transcend physical limitations. His journey from prisoner to president reflects the profound impact of Stoic resilience, showing that true freedom lies not in external circumstances but in the mastery of one's mind.

3. Maya Angelou: The Poet's Journey from Trauma to Liberation

Maya Angelou, renowned poet, and civil rights activist, used Epictetus' philosophy as a tool for personal healing and mental liberation. Growing up in a segregated society, Angelou faced numerous challenges, including racial discrimination, abuse, and trauma. For years, she struggled with feelings of powerlessness and fear, yet she ultimately reclaimed her freedom by focusing on her inner life, cultivating resilience, and finding her voice.

In her writings, Angelou reflects on the transformative power of acceptance and resilience, both core Stoic principles. She once said, "You may not control all the events that happen to you, but you can decide not to be reduced by them." Angelou's journey of mental liberation illustrates Epictetus' teaching that while we may not control external events, we have the power to shape our responses and define our own worth. By embracing her own resilience, Angelou transformed her pain into poetry, using her experiences to inspire others and advocate for social change.

Practical Application: Exercises for Mental Liberation

Epictetus' teachings on mental freedom can be applied in everyday life, offering tools for cultivating resilience, acceptance, and inner peace. The following exercises are designed to help readers experience mental liberation, regardless of their external circumstances.

The "Letting Go" List Begin by making a list of worries or challenges that you currently face. Divide the list into two columns: "Within My Control" and "Beyond My Control." In the "Within My Control" column, list actions you can take, attitudes you can adjust, or choices you can make. In the "Beyond My Control" column, list external events, other people's actions, or outcomes that are outside your influence. Once you've completed the list, take a few moments to reflect on how much energy you've spent trying to control things that lie outside your influence. Make a conscious decision to release these concerns, focusing only on what you can control. This exercise helps reinforce Epictetus' teaching on mental freedom by directing your energy toward areas where you can make a difference, freeing you from the mental burden of trying to control the uncontrollable.

Daily Resilience Reflection Each day, take five minutes to reflect on a challenging situation you encountered. Ask yourself: How did I respond? What thoughts or actions were within my control? How did I handle what I couldn't control? By practicing this reflection, you can develop greater awareness of your own responses, fostering a sense of inner freedom and resilience. Over time, this exercise builds mental discipline, helping you to approach life's challenges with greater calm and clarity.

Visualization of Inner Freedom Find a quiet place to sit and close your eyes. Take a few deep breaths, then visualize yourself in a challenging situation. Imagine that you are surrounded by obstacles or limitations. Now, shift your focus inward, picturing a light or calm presence within you that remains unaffected by these external constraints. Visualize yourself standing strong, grounded in your values and inner peace, even as difficulties arise. Repeat to yourself, "My freedom lies within," reinforcing your belief in your own mental strength. This visualization helps anchor you in the idea that true freedom is internal, unshaken by external forces.

The Global Relevance of Epictetus' Teachings on Freedom

Epictetus' philosophy of mental freedom has resonated across cultures and generations, inspiring movements for social and political liberation. His teachings offer a powerful message for those who face oppression, discrimination, or adversity, encouraging individuals to reclaim their agency by focusing on what lies within their control. In modern contexts, his ideas have influenced prison reform, social justice initiatives, and therapeutic practices that empower individuals to transcend external limitations.

For example, prison reform programs inspired by Stoic philosophy have introduced inmates to Stoic teachings as a means of fostering inner freedom. These programs encourage individuals to cultivate resilience and self-discipline, emphasizing that while their physical freedom may be restricted, their mental freedom is within their control. By embracing Epictetus' teachings, participants learn to approach their circumstances with acceptance and purpose, discovering a sense of freedom that no prison walls can contain.

Epictetus' insights are also relevant for social justice activists who work toward a more just society. By focusing on their own actions, values, and purpose, activists can sustain their commitment to change without being overwhelmed by frustration or burnout. His teachings encourage individuals to act with integrity and resilience, creating a foundation of mental strength that supports long-term social and political efforts.

Conclusion: The Path to Inner Freedom

Epictetus' philosophy of mental liberation offers a pathway to true freedom, one that transcends external conditions and empowers individuals to master their own minds. His teachings remind us that while we may not control the world around us, we can control our own responses, finding peace, resilience, and strength within. By embracing this concept of inner freedom, we open ourselves to a life of purpose and authenticity, guided not by the pursuit of external power but by the cultivation of inner strength.

In a world filled with challenges, Epictetus' message is both timeless and transformative. He teaches us that freedom begins in the mind, and that by mastering our thoughts, emotions, and actions, we can live with a sense of peace and purpose that no external force can diminish. His philosophy of freedom invites each of us to step into our own power, to face life's challenges with courage and resilience, and to find within ourselves a source of liberation that endures.

Bonus Chapter Six

A Day in the Life of Epictetus' School—Immersing Readers in the Ancient World of Stoic Training

In Nicopolis, a coastal town in ancient Greece, Epictetus' school thrived as a place of deep thought, discipline, and wisdom. His students came from far and wide to study Stoicism under the former slave turned philosopher who taught not only through words but through example, guiding his followers to embody Stoic principles in every aspect of life. A day in Epictetus' school was not simply about absorbing ideas but about living those ideas, allowing them to transform each student from within.

This chapter brings to life what a typical day might have looked like for a student in Epictetus' school. From the first light of dawn to the closing discussions at dusk, we will journey through the daily routine of a Stoic student, feel the impact of Epictetus' teaching techniques, and engage with the exercises and dialogues that made his school a sanctuary for the mind and spirit. Here, in the stillness of ancient Greece, amid marble columns and sunlit courtyards, we will discover what it truly meant to study Stoicism under one of its most influential teachers.

The Daily Routine of a Stoic Student

As the sun's first light breaks over the horizon, students rise from their simple cots. The school is austere, embodying the Stoic belief that true happiness lies not in luxury but in living with virtue. Each morning begins in silence. The students, mostly young men and a few women, gather in the courtyard. Their clothing is simple, as is the sparse stone setting around them. They sit cross-legged on the cool ground, inhaling the crisp morning air, and prepare their minds for the day ahead.

Meditation is the first practice of the morning. Epictetus has taught his students to greet each day with reflection, to consider what lies within their control and what does not. In silence, they contemplate the inevitable challenges they will face and remind themselves that their thoughts and actions are the only true domains of influence. They meditate on questions like, "What am I prepared to endure?" and "How will I remain steadfast?" In this space of quiet introspection, they strengthen their resolve to meet life's hardships with courage and clarity.

After meditation, the students rise and proceed to a small dining area for a simple breakfast of bread, olives, and figs. Conversations are subdued but thoughtful. Here, even a casual word can spark a lesson, as Epictetus encourages his students to observe their thoughts and be mindful in every action. Mealtime, for Stoics, is as much a practice in moderation and gratitude as it is about nourishing the body. The students are mindful of their intake, understanding that excess of any kind—whether in food or thought—clouds the mind and hinders clear reasoning.

After breakfast, they gather in the main teaching hall. Epictetus stands at the front, his presence calm but commanding. His students sit attentively, ready to learn not just philosophy but a way of life.

Stoic Exercises and Dialogues

Epictetus' teaching style is immersive and interactive. He does not merely lecture; he engages his students in dialogue, guiding them to their own realizations through questions. A typical lesson might begin with a student sharing a recent struggle—perhaps frustration over a perceived injustice or the disappointment of unfulfilled hopes. Epictetus listens intently, then poses questions to steer the student toward insight.

On this particular morning, a young student named Leander raises a concern. "Master, I am often troubled by the actions of my brother. He makes unwise choices and has been drawn to pursuits that I find wasteful and even harmful. I have tried speaking with him, but he ignores my advice. How can I remain unaffected by his actions?"

Epictetus nods, aware of the common struggle to influence loved ones. "Tell me, Leander," he begins, "whose choices do you have power over—yours or your brother's?"

Leander hesitates. "Only mine, Master."

"Then why do you waste your peace on what is beyond your control?" Epictetus' tone is firm but compassionate. "Consider this: if you pour your energy into fretting over another's actions, you are abandoning the very power you do have—your own thoughts, your own actions, your own virtue."

The other students listen closely as Leander processes this. "But what if his actions bring harm?"

Epictetus replies with a lesson on accepting what one cannot change. "You may show him a better way through your own example, but you cannot make him follow it. If you wish to be free, you must release your attachment to outcomes beyond your influence. Peace lies not in controlling others, but in mastering yourself."

He pauses, letting the weight of the lesson settle. The students sense the depth of this truth, recognizing that Epictetus is not just speaking to Leander but to all of them. The struggle to influence loved ones, to change things that lie beyond control, is a universal challenge. By relinquishing this need for control, they understand, they can reclaim their inner freedom.

After this exchange, Epictetus introduces a Stoic exercise known as *premeditatio malorum*, or the "pre-meditation of evils." He instructs the students to imagine the various challenges they might face throughout the day: a harsh word, a disappointment, an unforeseen delay. He encourages them to mentally prepare for these difficulties, reminding themselves that they have the power to respond with patience and equanimity.

"Imagine that you encounter an insult today," he says, looking around at each student. "How will you respond?"

A student named Cassius responds, "With calm, Master. For I know that the insult speaks more of the person who says it than of me."

Epictetus smiles. "Indeed. When you anticipate challenges, you are less likely to be caught off guard. Prepare yourself mentally for the day's trials, and when they come, you will find that they do not disturb you as they once did."

The students nod, internalizing this practice. By envisioning potential hardships, they are better equipped to face them with a Stoic resolve, viewing adversity not as a threat but as an opportunity to practice their philosophy.

Epictetus' Teaching Techniques

Epictetus is known not just for his wisdom but for his unique approach to teaching. Unlike other philosophers who might rely solely on lectures, Epictetus engages his students through Socratic questioning, dialogue, and real-life application. His goal is not to impart knowledge for its own sake, but to inspire his students to live in accordance with Stoic principles.

Epictetus often employs stories to illustrate his points, drawing from his own experiences as a former slave. "I was once like many of you," he tells them, "bound by desires, by anger, by the hope that others might change. But I discovered that freedom does not lie in external circumstances. True freedom lies here," he says, pointing to his heart. "It is the unshakable strength that comes from within."

The students listen, captivated not just by his words but by the authenticity behind them. Epictetus' past as a slave is not merely a story; it is a testament to the power of Stoic principles to transform suffering into strength. His teachings carry a weight that no abstract philosophy can match, as they are rooted in his lived experience.

In addition to storytelling, Epictetus often incorporates practical exercises into his lessons. One such exercise involves *ethos*—the cultivation of moral character. He instructs his students to spend each evening reflecting on their actions of the day, examining whether they lived in alignment with their values. This exercise, he explains, is essential for developing the habit of self-discipline and integrity.

"Ask yourselves each night," he advises, "Did I act with wisdom today? Did I seek virtue above comfort? Did I respond to others with compassion?" By cultivating this habit, his students learn to hold themselves accountable, strengthening their commitment to Stoic principles.

Afternoon Philosophical Discourse

As midday approaches, the students take a break from their lessons to gather in the shade of the courtyard for a simple meal. Afterward, they return to the teaching hall, where Epictetus leads them in a philosophical discourse. Today's topic is the nature of freedom.

"Many people believe that freedom comes from wealth, power, or social status," Epictetus begins. "But these things are external, and thus, they are fragile. True freedom lies not in what we own, but in our ability to govern our own minds."

One student, Theo, raises his hand. "But Master, can we truly be free if we live under a tyrant or are bound by poverty?"

Epictetus' gaze is steady. "Imagine that you are imprisoned," he says. "Your body may be confined, but your mind remains your own. You have the power to choose your thoughts, to cultivate peace, to live in harmony with virtue. That is a freedom that no one can take from you."

The students sit in thoughtful silence, absorbing this profound truth. Epictetus has shown them that while external freedom is valuable, it is not essential for inner peace. Even those who live under oppression or hardship can cultivate a freedom that surpasses physical constraints. This concept of mental liberation resonates deeply, inspiring the students to pursue a form of freedom that is unbreakable, unassailable by the world's injustices.

Evening Reflections and the Value of Virtue

As the day draws to a close, the students gather once more in the hall for evening reflections. Epictetus leads them in a final discussion, encouraging each student to share what they have learned. One by one, they speak of the day's lessons—the practice of letting go, the resilience in the face of insults, the cultivation of inner freedom.

"Remember," Epictetus tells them, "that philosophy is not an ornament but a shield. It is not something you wear for show, but something that protects you in the storms of life. To be a Stoic is to live with courage, humility, and a deep reverence for the nature of things."

In the softening light, the students reflect on his words, each feeling a quiet strength kindled within them. They understand that Stoicism is not a path to escape life's difficulties but a means of facing them with grace. Through Epictetus' guidance, they have glimpsed the power of a life lived in accordance with nature, a life anchored in virtue, compassion, and self-mastery.

As they leave the hall and retire to their quarters, each student carries with them a renewed commitment to the Stoic path. They are not merely learning philosophy; they are becoming Stoics, embodying the teachings of Epictetus in every thought, word, and deed.

Closing Reflections

A day in Epictetus' school is more than a series of lessons; it is an immersion in a way of life that seeks to transcend the transient, to embrace the eternal principles of wisdom and virtue. Through meditation, dialogue, and self-reflection, Epictetus' students learn to cultivate a freedom that comes from within, a freedom that no external force can diminish.

For the modern reader, this day in Epictetus' school offers a glimpse into the origins of Stoicism, a journey into the mind of a philosopher who taught not for prestige but for transformation. Epictetus' teachings endure because they are not mere abstractions; they are living truths, a guide for anyone seeking to master themselves and live with purpose.

In a world of change and uncertainty, Epictetus invites us to find stability within. To his students, he offers not only knowledge but a path to liberation, a way to live in harmony with both the world and oneself. Through his school, we are reminded that true wisdom is timeless, and that each of us, in our own lives, can choose the path of the Stoic.

Bonus Chapter Seven

Epictetus' Legacy Through Art, Literature, and Culture

The teachings of Epictetus have shaped the foundation of Stoic thought, offering principles of inner freedom and resilience that extend far beyond philosophy. His ideas have permeated the worlds of literature, art, music, and even popular culture, cementing his legacy as a symbol of personal liberation and enduring strength. From Renaissance literature to modern-day novels, from classical music to motivational movements, Epictetus' influence has rippled through centuries, inspiring countless artists, writers, and thinkers to explore the boundaries of human resilience and the transformative power of self-mastery.

Epictetus' philosophy teaches that freedom is an internal state, a mastery of one's thoughts and responses that cannot be shaken by external circumstances. This idea has resonated with generations of artists and writers who sought to express the indomitable spirit of humanity. In this chapter, we will explore how Epictetus' teachings have left an indelible mark on Western culture, tracing his influence through literature, art, music, and contemporary media. Through these cultural expressions, we find that Stoic themes of freedom, resilience, and self-discipline are not only philosophical ideals but also sources of inspiration that have enriched human creativity.

Literary Impact: Epictetus in the World of Letters

Epictetus' influence on literature spans centuries, from the Renaissance to Romanticism, and into the realms of contemporary novels and poetry. His ideas on freedom and resilience have captivated authors, offering a framework through which characters can confront hardship and grow. The Stoic theme of inner strength, which holds that true freedom lies in one's own mind, has become a recurrent motif in Western literature, where protagonists often embody the struggle to master their inner world amidst external turmoil.

During the Renaissance, Stoic ideas enjoyed a revival as scholars and writers sought ancient sources of wisdom to navigate a rapidly changing world. Renaissance humanists, captivated by the teachings of Epictetus, drew upon his philosophy to emphasize individual agency and self-reliance. Michel de Montaigne, the French essayist, was particularly influenced by Epictetus' teachings. Montaigne, whose essays are infused with Stoic themes, wrote on the importance of self-examination and the acceptance of life's inevitable hardships. For Montaigne, as for Epictetus, the path to freedom lay in understanding one's own mind and embracing life's uncertainties with grace.

In the Romantic period, Epictetus' philosophy found resonance with writers who explored the power of the human spirit to transcend suffering. The English poet William Wordsworth, known for his reflections on nature and the human experience, echoed Stoic ideas in his verse, emphasizing resilience and self-reflection. Wordsworth's poetry celebrates the strength of the human mind to find peace amidst life's trials, a theme that aligns with Epictetus' belief that true freedom is found within. Similarly, the works of Johann Wolfgang von Goethe, particularly in *Faust*, explore the inner struggle for meaning and liberation, drawing on Stoic principles to illustrate the journey of self-mastery.

In contemporary literature, Stoic themes continue to shape characters and narratives that focus on resilience. Viktor Frankl, a Holocaust survivor and psychiatrist, referenced Epictetus in his seminal work, *Man's Search for Meaning*. Frankl's philosophy, developed during his imprisonment in Nazi concentration camps, reflects Epictetus' teaching that while we cannot control our circumstances, we have power over our response to them. Frankl's emphasis on finding purpose in suffering is a modern reflection of Epictetus' belief in the transformative power of acceptance and mental discipline.

Even in fiction, Epictetus' philosophy appears as a source of inner strength. Novels like *The Road* by Cormac McCarthy, which tells the story of a father and son navigating a desolate world, echo Stoic ideas of resilience and moral integrity. The protagonists' struggle to maintain hope and compassion in a bleak world resonates with Epictetus' teaching that true strength lies in how we choose to face adversity. These literary explorations of Stoic themes reveal that Epictetus' influence is far-reaching, inspiring authors to create characters who embody the quest for freedom through self-mastery.

Artistic and Musical Interpretations: Stoicism on Canvas and in Sound

Beyond literature, Epictetus' teachings have also inspired artists and composers to explore Stoic themes through visual art and music. The art world, especially during the Renaissance, often depicted scenes that evoked Stoic principles, reflecting society's fascination with philosophy as a guide for life. Paintings of philosophers, as well as allegorical works that emphasize resilience and inner strength, serve as visual representations of Stoic ideals, bringing Epictetus' message to life in forms that engage the eye and the spirit.

One of the most notable Stoic-inspired artworks is Raphael's *The School of Athens*, a fresco that represents an ideal gathering of ancient philosophers, including Epictetus' fellow Stoic, Zeno of Citium. Though Epictetus is not specifically depicted, the painting celebrates the intellectual legacy of Stoicism, capturing the contemplative spirit of philosophers who sought wisdom beyond worldly desires. The figures in *The School of Athens* embody the Stoic ideal of individuals in pursuit of knowledge, transcending the distractions of the material world to engage in philosophical inquiry.

Music, too, has explored Stoic themes, with composers drawing on Epictetus' teachings to express inner resilience and moral integrity. Ludwig van Beethoven, for example, admired the Stoic philosophy, finding solace in its principles during his struggle with deafness. Beethoven's later works, especially his Ninth Symphony, are imbued with a profound sense of triumph over adversity. The famous *Ode to Joy* movement, which celebrates human resilience and unity, echoes Stoic themes of inner strength and collective harmony, reflecting Beethoven's belief in the power of the human spirit to transcend suffering.

In the modern era, music continues to explore Stoic themes, with artists across genres drawing on Epictetus' philosophy to express resilience and self-empowerment. Jazz musician John

Coltrane, whose music reflects a journey of personal and spiritual transformation, embodied the Stoic ideal of self-mastery and resilience. Coltrane's later works, which are introspective and experimental, reveal his commitment to personal growth and spiritual exploration, themes that align closely with Stoic teachings.

Through visual art and music, Epictetus' legacy extends into creative expressions that capture the beauty of resilience. These artistic interpretations allow audiences to experience Stoic ideas in ways that resonate beyond intellectual understanding, evoking emotional and aesthetic appreciation for the strength of the human spirit.

Modern Cultural Reflections: Epictetus in Popular Culture and Mindfulness Movements

Today, Epictetus' influence can be found not only in traditional art forms but also in popular culture, where his teachings on freedom and resilience have inspired everything from motivational quotes to mindfulness movements. In a world marked by constant change and uncertainty, Epictetus' philosophy offers a source of stability, encouraging individuals to find peace within themselves regardless of external circumstances.

One of the most significant modern reflections of Epictetus' philosophy is the rise of mindfulness practices, which emphasize self-awareness, acceptance, and inner peace. Mindfulness shares many principles with Stoicism, particularly the focus on living in the present and accepting what lies beyond one's control. Mindfulness practitioners, like Stoics, cultivate the ability to observe their thoughts without attachment, finding freedom in letting go of unnecessary desires and judgments. This approach aligns closely with Epictetus' teaching that inner freedom is achieved by mastering one's mind, making Stoic philosophy highly relevant for today's mindfulness and wellness communities.

In addition to mindfulness, motivational speakers and self-help authors frequently reference Stoic teachings, often including quotes from Epictetus in their messages of resilience and empowerment. Phrases like "It's not what happens to you, but how you react to it that matters," attributed to Epictetus, have become popular mantras for those seeking strength and clarity in challenging times. These quotes, which circulate widely on social media and in self-help literature, reflect the enduring appeal of Stoic wisdom as a guide for personal growth and resilience.

Epictetus' teachings have even made their way into contemporary films, where characters often embody Stoic principles of self-control and inner peace. In movies like *The Pursuit of Happyness*, which follows the journey of a man overcoming extreme hardship, audiences witness the power of resilience and inner strength—qualities that Epictetus emphasized. Characters who embody Stoic virtues inspire viewers to cultivate their own inner freedom, reminding them that true strength lies not in external achievements but in the ability to remain grounded amidst life's ups and downs.

Exercises in Cultural Reflection: Engaging with Epictetus' Legacy

To help readers connect with Epictetus' legacy in culture, the following exercises encourage reflection on Stoic principles through engagement with art, literature, and modern media.

Literary Reflection on Resilience Choose a novel, poem, or play that explores themes of resilience or self-mastery. As you read, consider how the characters embody Stoic principles. Reflect on their journey, noting moments when they exercise inner strength in the face of adversity. After reading, write a short reflection on how the story relates to Epictetus' teachings, considering what lessons you can apply in your own life.

Art as a Meditation on Stoicism Visit an art museum or gallery, or explore famous artworks online, focusing on pieces that evoke calm, resilience, or contemplation. As you observe each artwork, ask yourself: What feelings does this piece evoke? How does it relate to the idea of inner freedom? Use this experience as a meditation on Stoicism, allowing the artwork to serve as a visual reminder of your own inner strength.

Music and Mindfulness Create a playlist of music that embodies themes of resilience, peace, and inner strength. As you listen, practice mindfulness by focusing on the emotions each piece evokes, allowing yourself to connect with the music's message of resilience. Reflect on how these themes relate to Epictetus' philosophy, considering ways to cultivate this mindset in your daily life.

Contemporary Media Reflection Choose a film, podcast, or documentary that features themes of self-mastery, resilience, or personal growth. Afterward, reflect on how the message aligns with Epictetus' teachings. Consider how the characters or speakers respond to challenges, and what insights you can draw for your own journey. This exercise allows you to explore Stoicism through modern perspectives, deepening your understanding of Epictetus' influence on contemporary culture.

Conclusion: Epictetus' Timeless Influence on the Human Spirit

Epictetus' legacy in art, literature, music, and popular culture demonstrates the universal appeal of his philosophy. His teachings on inner freedom, resilience, and self-mastery have transcended time and medium, inspiring countless individuals to seek peace and strength within themselves. By engaging with Epictetus' legacy in these creative forms, we find that his philosophy is not confined to the pages of ancient texts; it lives on in the stories we tell, the art we create, and the music we cherish.

Through the lens of Epictetus' teachings, we are reminded that each of us has the power to cultivate our own inner freedom. His influence encourages us to explore the boundaries of resilience, to find beauty in the pursuit of wisdom, and to recognize that true strength lies in mastering our own minds. As we engage with Epictetus' legacy, we are invited not only to learn from his philosophy but to live it, embracing the transformative power of inner freedom.

Closing Chapter

The Inner Throne of Freedom

As we reach the close of our journey through the life and wisdom of Epictetus, it becomes clear that his teachings transcend time, geography, and circumstance. Epictetus began life as a slave and rose to become one of the most influential philosophers of his age. His story is not merely a testament to Stoic philosophy; it's a call to action for all who seek to live with greater purpose, resilience, and inner peace. Epictetus believed that freedom was not something that could be granted or taken away by others; it was an internal state, accessible to all who cultivate the strength of mind to claim it. Through his words and teachings, he has gifted us a path to inner freedom—a freedom that, once understood, can never be lost.

Epictetus' journey reminds us that adversity is not an obstacle to be feared but an opportunity to be embraced. In a world where hardship is often seen as an impediment, Epictetus teaches us to view challenges as powerful instructors. He faced exile, limitation, and hardship, yet he emerged not broken, but strengthened by these experiences. His response to adversity was not bitterness or retreat, but wisdom and courage. His life urges us to reflect: How do we react when we face difficulty? Do we shrink back, or do we rise, using each challenge as an opportunity to develop our character?

This question is central to Epictetus' teachings and remains profoundly relevant to our own lives. Today's world is rife with distractions and anxieties—challenges that, while different in form from those Epictetus faced, still require the same mental clarity and strength. In an age where so many strive for external success, Epictetus reminds us that true mastery is found within. When we learn to govern our minds, to direct our thoughts and actions in alignment with our values, we gain a freedom that no circumstance can take away. This freedom, grounded in self-mastery, is the foundation of a fulfilling life. It is the essence of Stoic resilience.

Epictetus taught that while we may not control the events that unfold around us, we always have power over our responses. This is a teaching that carries within it both responsibility and liberation. It means that our peace, our happiness, and our fulfillment are ours to create. We are not at the mercy of external forces; we are the authors of our experience. This power to choose our response is the true gift of Epictetus' philosophy, a reminder that no matter the challenge, we hold the key to our own freedom.

Reflecting on Epictetus' life, we are invited to ask ourselves: What does freedom mean to us? Is it wealth, status, or the absence of difficulty? Or is it something deeper—an internal state that remains steady and unshaken no matter what life may bring? Epictetus believed that freedom is a state of mind, a strength of character that is cultivated through self-discipline and wisdom. This freedom, he taught, is available to each of us, regardless of our circumstances. It is a freedom that empowers us to live in harmony with our values, to face life's trials with courage, and to find peace within ourselves.

The legacy of Epictetus is not just his philosophy, but the invitation to make his teachings a living part of our lives. He challenges us to practice resilience, to cultivate gratitude, to embrace acceptance, and to live with integrity. These principles are not abstract ideals; they are practical tools that we can use each day to build a life of purpose and meaning. Epictetus reminds us that wisdom is not found in avoiding life's challenges but in engaging with them fully, in using each moment as an opportunity to grow in strength, clarity, and understanding.

As we leave the pages of this book, we carry with us Epictetus' teachings not as memories of a distant philosopher but as guides for our own journey. His words become our companions in moments of uncertainty, his wisdom a steadying force when life seems overwhelming. Epictetus has shown us that freedom, resilience, and peace are not gifts that others can bestow upon us; they are the fruits of our own dedication, our own commitment to live in alignment with our values.

To live as Epictetus taught is to live with courage, to choose strength over complacency, and to find freedom in the mastery of our own minds. In embracing this philosophy, we discover that true freedom is not about what we have or what we achieve, but about who we choose to become. Epictetus has shown us that the path to freedom begins within, and it is a path open to each of us, no matter where we begin or what challenges we may face. This is the ultimate gift of his legacy: the knowledge that we, too, can be free.

Enduring Wisdom

The freedom Epictetus spoke of is not distant or unreachable. It lies within us, waiting to be claimed by those who seek to live with purpose, strength, and resilience. Through his life, Epictetus showed us that we are capable of much more than we might realize, that our minds are our most powerful tools, and that our freedom is always within reach. As we carry these lessons forward, may we find the courage to live with integrity, the strength to face adversity with grace, and the wisdom to seek freedom not in the world around us but in the depths of our own hearts and minds.

This closing chapter, *The Slave Who Freed Kings,* encapsulates the essence of Epictetus' teachings and leaves readers with an inspiring, lasting message that they can apply to their own lives.

Thank you for allowing me to share this journey with you.

With deep gratitude,

Natalie Larsen/Oliver Michaels

Historic Context and Manuscript Legacy

Language and Writing:

Epictetus, a former slave who became one of Stoicism's most revered teachers, spoke primarily in Greek, the language of philosophy and intellectual life during his time. His profound insights, transcribed by his student Arrian in *The Discourses* and *The Enchiridion*, became the foundation for Stoic thought and laid a philosophical path that later guided great minds, including Marcus Aurelius. Epictetus' use of Greek was deliberate, as he sought to convey the universal ideals of Stoicism in the language that was most associated with philosophical discourse.

Although Marcus Aurelius was a Roman emperor and fluent in Latin, he chose to write his personal reflections, *Meditations*, in Greek, a testament to the influence Greek philosophy had on his intellectual and personal life. This decision also reflects the respect he held for the Stoic tradition pioneered by thinkers like Epictetus. Greek, with its rich philosophical vocabulary, enabled Marcus to explore Stoic concepts in depth and precision. Epictetus' teachings directly inspired Marcus' contemplative approach to life and leadership, providing a model for applying Stoic principles in moments of personal and political adversity.

In *Meditations*, Marcus wrote phrases like, "We live only now. Everything else is either passed or is unknown." In Greek, this passage reads:

"Μόνο τώρα ζούμε. Όλα τα υπόλοιπα είτε έχουν περάσει είτε είναι άγνωστα." — *Marcus Aurelius*

This translation captures the philosophical tone and immediacy of the original Greek, a language deeply associated with wisdom and reflection in the ancient world. The influence of Epictetus' philosophy is evident in these reflections, underscoring Marcus' belief in the present moment as the only time under our control—a core tenet he inherited from Epictetus.

Manuscripts and Early Copies:

Meditations was written in Greek, under the title Τὰ εἰς ἑαυτόν (*Ta eis heauton*), meaning "To Himself." The work consists of personal reflections meant for his own guidance rather than for publication.

Surviving Manuscripts:

Codex Palatinus 398 (9th-10th century):

One of the earliest surviving manuscripts of *Meditations*, written in Greek, housed in the Vatican Library.

Codex Vaticanus Graecus 1950 (14th century):

Another significant manuscript located in the Vatican Library.

Codex Trecensis 581 (10th century):

This manuscript is kept in the Bibliothèque Nationale in Paris.

Printed Editions:

Editio Princeps (1558): The first printed edition of *Meditations* was published in Zurich by the humanist scholar Xylander (Wilhelm Holtzmann). This edition reintroduced Marcus Aurelius' thoughts to the Western world during the Renaissance.

Modern Translations: Numerous translations exist today, based on these and other manuscripts, making Marcus Aurelius' *Meditations* widely accessible in many languages.

Availability and Access:

Many ancient manuscripts are held in major libraries and archives, such as the Vatican Library and the Bibliothèque Nationale. Some have been digitized and are accessible online through scholarly databases or library websites.

Loeb Classical Library: This well-known series of books provides the Greek text of *Meditations* alongside an English translation, making the work accessible to both scholars and general readers.

These early manuscripts and editions have allowed scholars to study the text and its transmission over centuries, offering insights into the philosophical ideas of Marcus Aurelius and the Stoic tradition.

This layout provides a clear, organized structure for your section, helping readers understand the historical and linguistic context of Marcus Aurelius' *Meditations* and where they can find these important manuscripts.

If you're interested in reading or accessing the manuscripts of Marcus Aurelius' *Meditations*, here are some ways to do so:

1. Major Libraries and Archives

Vatican Library (Bibliotheca Apostolica Vaticana):

Codex Palatinus 398 and Codex Vaticanus Graecus 1950 are housed here. The Vatican Library holds one of the most significant collections of ancient manuscripts, including those of *Meditations*. While the library is not open to the general public, scholars and researchers can request access.

Bibliothèque Nationale de France (BnF):

The Codex Trecensis 581 is kept here. The BnF in Paris is one of the world's largest libraries, and it preserves numerous historical manuscripts. Access is generally restricted to researchers, but some items have been digitized and are available online.

2. Online Digital Libraries

Vatican Library Digital Archives:

Some of the Vatican's manuscript collections have been digitized and made available online. You can explore their digital archive to view these ancient texts.

Gallica (BnF Digital Library):

Gallica is the digital library of the BnF and provides access to a wide range of digitized manuscripts, including ancient texts like those of Marcus Aurelius.

3. Scholarly Databases

Perseus Digital Library:

Hosted by Tufts University, Perseus offers a collection of ancient texts, including Greek and Latin works, with translations. While it might not have the original manuscript images, it provides reliable texts and translations.

Internet Archive:

The Internet Archive has digitized versions of many old and rare books, including early editions of *Meditations*. While these may not be original manuscripts, they can offer insight into how the text has been preserved and interpreted over time.

4. Published Editions and Translations

Loeb Classical Library:

The Loeb Classical Library publishes bilingual editions of ancient texts, including *Meditations*. Each book provides the Greek text alongside an English translation, making it accessible for both scholarly study and general reading.

5. Visiting the Libraries

Research Visits:

If you're a scholar or have a specific research project, you may be able to arrange a visit to view these manuscripts in person. This usually requires a formal application process, proof of academic credentials, and a detailed research proposal.

These resources offer different ways to access and study the manuscripts of *Meditations*, whether you're looking for a digital experience or planning a more traditional research visit.

In the original writings of Marcus Aurelius, such as those found in *Meditations*, he would not have used quotation marks as we do in modern writing. Quotation marks are a relatively recent development in the history of writing, becoming common in European languages during the Renaissance and later. Ancient Greek texts, including those written by Marcus Aurelius, were written without punctuation marks like quotation marks.

If Marcus Aurelius had written the quote "Everything we hear is an opinion, not a fact. Everything we see is a perspective, not the truth." in Greek, it would likely have appeared as continuous text without any punctuation to denote the beginning or end of a quote. Here's how it might have looked in ancient Greek, based on the style of the time:

Original Greek Text:

Πᾶν ὅ τι ἀκούομεν δόξα ἐστίν, οὐκ ἀλήθεια. Πᾶν ὅ τι βλέπομεν ὀπτική ἐστίν, οὐκ ἀλήθεια.

Explanation:

No Quotation Marks: The text would be written as a straightforward statement without quotation marks.

No Punctuation or Diacritics: Ancient Greek manuscripts often lacked the punctuation and diacritical marks (like accents) that are used in modern editions of ancient texts. The text would flow continuously, often without breaks even between sentences. In early manuscripts, this text might have been written in scriptio continua (continuous script), where words run together without spaces between them, though by the time of Marcus Aurelius, spacing between words was more common. Still, the lack of punctuation, including quotation marks, was typical.

Example in Scriptio Continua:

ΠΑΝΟΤΙΑΚΟΥΟΜΕΝΔΟΞΑΕΣΤΙΝΟΥΚΑΛΗΘΕΙΑΠΑΝΟΤ ΙΒΛΕΠΟΜΕΝΟΠΤΙΚΗΕΣΤΙΝΟΥΚΑΛΗΘΕΙΑ

This format reflects the ancient style of writing, which relied on the reader's familiarity with the language and context to understand the structure and meaning. The lack of modern punctuation meant that emphasis and interpretation were often guided by the reader's own understanding and the flow of the text.

www.ingramcontent.com/pod-product-compliance
Lightning Source LLC
Chambersburg PA
CBHW021127070726
47591CB00014B/1681